COLLISIONS

violences by Jack Foley

COLLISIONS

violences by Jack Foley

Academica Press
Washington~London

Library of Congress Cataloging-in-Publication Data

Names: Foley, Jack (author)
Title: Collisions : violences | Foley, Jack.
Description: Washington : Academica Press, 2024. | Includes references.
Identifiers: LCCN 2024938401 | ISBN 9781680533354 (hardcover) |
9781680533361 (paperback) | 9781680533378 (e-book)

For my dear ones, Sean, Kerry & Sangye
and to the memory of my late wife, Adelle.

And to the spirit of William Butler Yeats.

...

Cover Design: Paul Veres

FOR PAOLO

"Mr. Foley!"
"Mr. Veres!"
and conversation began.
we met because
you had designed a book
for the artist, Helen Breger.
it was my assignment
to write verses
for the book.
later, when I was sick,
barely able to walk,
you looked at me,
and said, "You poor man"
and took me to your chiropractor.
later still, the chiropractor phoned
when you were in the hospital
on your deathbed.
you said wryly,
"No adjustment this week."
"That's Paul," said the chiropractor.
I remember you wept
when you spoke of Adelle
at a gathering for me.
marvelous artist,
you took the best photo
of Sangye and me
anyone has ever taken
or is ever likely to take—
naturally taken
at a Vietnamese restaurant—
and the three
book covers you made for me
are wonders.
I remember
that you were excited
when one of your fonts

was used on the cover
of Harper Lee's
Go Set a Watchman
(you were 71 then):
much earlier,
you had named the font
for your mother.
and you told me about
your older brother
but never told me
his name. (Peter.)
how many lunches
did we have,
usually at restaurants
of my choice—Vietnamese.
you were addicted to bad—
no, dreadful—
jokes.
("I made that one up.")
it was part
of your charm,
the child
that never left you.
dear man:
have you heard the one about
birds?
about how you died
at exactly the time
when they make
their vast
migrations outward.
for the ancients
birds and souls
were the same.
is it possible
that amid the weeping
of your many friends,
whose desolation was deep
as you lay dying
(you helped so many),
you secretly
grew wings,
vast, scarlet ones,
showy wings
that no one else saw,

and while friends wept
you quietly left the hospital
and joined
that monumental avian dislocation.
was that a last
joke?
fly free
dear friend,
you were a good man
and did many good things
for the world.
I hear your laughter
in the clamor
of the wind.

Paul Veres, June 21, 1944-May 3, 2024

CONTENTS

A conventional myth of modern society is that the individual possesses a unified consciousness. A personality is assumed to be a single entity in which all the parts form an indivisible whole. Contemporary neuroscience has demonstrated that this notion is an illusion. Human consciousness is an unstable republic of conflicting impulses, instincts, and appetites in perpetual flux. Baudelaire understood or at least intuited this unsettling reality before the scientists and psychologists. His poems pull the reader into the confusion of his consciousness as experienced from the inside. Music was central to Baudelaire's method. He considered poetry an art of enchantment. 'A poem should cast a verbal spell that suspends the reader in a trance state of heightened attention and receptivity.' That momentary enchantment allows the reader to experience contradictory thoughts and emotions, to feel hidden suggestions and connections that are never fully disclosed or resolved in the poem.

—Dana Gioia, video essay: *Charles Baudelaire (Part 3): The Flowers of Evil*
https://www.youtube.com/watch?v=a4DNDUwXmgU&t=903s

•••

Nice playfulness with my calling you "revered" (reverend-ish is interesting in the sense that you certainly offer literature as a way to the spirit) but I like best your turning it into riverend, what I like about riverend is that it's the place the river empties into a lake or ocean, thus it moves into the mysteries, into the energies where all rivers are one…You are, to my mind, a seeker of more than we know.

— Rusty Morrison, email to Jack Foley

•••

no one
can live your death
for you,
said Heidegger.
know it
as intimately
as you know
your hands
your fingers
the touch
they make
on the skin
of your lover.
intimate, creative, violent death.

—Jack Foley

MR. SMITH GOES TO WASHINGTON: THE MOVIES

an introduction to this book

My girlfriend Sangye and I watched Frank Capra's amazing 1939 film, *Mr. Smith Goes to Washington*. Not the least amazing thing about it is the score by Dimitri Tiomkin: a constant presentation of American folk songs. It's a terrific, tear-inducing film, with marvelous performances by everyone. (It's said that Jean Arthur was so terrified of performing that she would vomit in her dressing room and then go in front of the camera and be absolutely perfect.)

Hard to deal with the emotional power of the film. I can't think of anyone who combines James Stewart's qualities of innocence, intelligence, honesty, and an endearing awkwardness that seems to suggest that everything about him is totally genuine. There's a terrific montage of Washington, DC monuments, places of interest at the beginning of the film that makes you want to join up! Just imagine: a thoroughly patriotic film that isn't jingoistic, that isn't something you can make fun of.

The director called these films Capra-corn, and so they are. Women are important in that world, they cheer you on and give you the very best advice, but it is a world of men and, especially, boys. (Stewart is called a "boy" several times in the film.) The moral is hooey, but it is deeply American hooey: the notion that a single man, a man like Lincoln, who shows up in the film via his statue in the Lincoln Monument, can combat the forces of greed and corruption and—though it may take almost every ounce of strength he has— can win, can overturn the bad guys who seem to have all the power in the world. I loved it and wept, even if I didn't exactly believe it. Movies! What magic they can perform. How they can make you believe that reality isn't real, that what you experience in the darkness of the theater, with men and women who have memorized lines and rehearsed the passions that seem so spontaneous, is far more genuine than what you know is true.

Sangye and I held hands throughout the film.

...

THE DANCE OF THE ROBOT SERVERS

they dance about the restaurant
they ask, Please tell me what you want
they move with grace and never run
beings from Kubrick's *2001*
they are not true but they're truly false
they cannot rhumba but oh, they waltz
these robowaitresses, robowaiters
who have no more hearts than refrigerators
pure servants who wish to serve—serve only
never tired, never lonely
never nervous, never drugged
(occasionally may come unplugged!)
no religion, no tortured soul
this is their dance—a barcarole:
they cannot walk but their wheels can roll
(they can't serve soup but they can serve sole)

MY CAREER IN THE ACADEMY:

A teacher,
Professor Gross-
vogel,
said:
"You
have a reputation
as a wild man,
Mr. Foley,
and while I may be
sympathetic
to that,
I'll mark
like a good
bourgeois."

He gave me an A.

BARBERSHOP
a dialogue

—Another way to conceive of consciousness in the manner that I think of it is to conceive of it as CHORDAL. This leads me to the strange possibility that in some ways the barbershop quartet is a better representation of consciousness than the solo singer.

—Singing "Sweet Adeline"!

— Singing anything—especially anything projecting a single protagonist. The great Buffalo Bills sing "If I Could Be With You One Hour Tonight." Their presentation begins, "If I could be," "If I could be," "If I could be," "If I could be"— one voice, one I, following another. What is I in that situation?

The song asserts a single protagonist but the single protagonist, the I, is represented by four different voices, each doing something different.

Consciousness is chordal.

How many meanings does Joyce's "Pass the fish for Christ's sake" have? Christ can be represented as a fish. He tells the disciples, "I will make you fishers of men." Is Joyce's line said in anger—"for Christ's sake" is an expletive—or in reverence, "for Christ's sake." Etc. Mightn't these various meanings be represented as voices?

—Yes! Like some of your poems!

—Probably like all of them!

...

READING O'NEILL

the hunger that besets me
daily the chaos around me
as large, imposing boxes accumulate & I

increasingly cannot
deal with them or
with the hunger which

I do not understand

ravenous, commanding hunger
which
is always asking

and the boxes
watch me with their
hungry eyes
& smile

& the green parrots
mock me with their language
unintelligible

in the rivers where my wandersoul
cries out

without hope
of the sea

COLLISIONS: AN ONGOING CHAOS

"Jack," said the much-published
Film critic to me
(After reading my lengthy,
Subtly-argued, not-yet-published
Paper citing Freud, Hegel, Baudelaire,
And various others—
And postulating "doubleness"
And the "Oedipus Complex")
"Jack, if all these things are in Hitchcock,
Why didn't *I* see them?"

madness is never far
in a Hitchcock film.
do you notice
what airline they take
when they go to Mount Rushmore
in *North by Northwest?*
—Northwest: they
go *north by Northwest.*

*

"I have always believed that you can reduce the Israeli-Palestinian conflict since the early 1900s to one line: conflict, timeout, conflict, timeout, conflict, timeout, conflict, timeout, conflict, timeout, conflict and timeout. The most important difference between the parties is what they each did during the timeouts.

"Israel built an impressive society and economy, even if flawed, and Hamas took nearly all of its resources and built attack tunnels."

   —Thomas L. Friedman, *NY Times*

"...as the Gaza death toll has climbed, and as Arab opinion has swung toward Hamas, the networks have seemingly capitulated to the feelings of their viewers. Putting aside 'the Hamas attack,' newscasters now increasingly refer to the Israeli 'war on Gaza.'"

   —David D. Kirkpatrick, Adam Rasgon, *The New Yorker*

SNUFF FILM

*Does the art of being a politician always end in justifying
(and perhaps enjoying) the murder of others? Look at the
expressions on the faces of President Obama and the others
as they watch video of the death of Osama bin Laden. (This
does not imply support for the policies of Osama bin Laden!)*

*

A prominent formalist poet asked me to write a blurb for his book of sonnets. I
wrote this:

Although the sonnet may not be the most
Fashionable of forms in these dark days,
There are the wondrous ones of Robert Frost
And others, who have entered its deep maze.

This "sonnetarium" of my friend L—
Is one example of the living form,
And there are others. At times I wonder who
Said sonnets were fit vittles for a worm.

With this key, T— unlocks his heart,
Engaging readers with these witty, passionate,
Unerring samples of a poet's art:
The sonnet!...Is there any cash in it?

Its branches grow and grow and are dendritic.
Just touch these suns. Scorn not the sonnet, Critic.

But printed it like this:

Although the sonnet may not be the most fashionable of forms in these dark
days, there are the wondrous ones of Robert Frost and others who have entered
its deep maze. This sonnetarium of my friend L— is one example of the living
form, and there are others. At times I wonder who said sonnets were fit vittles
for a worm. With this key T— unlocks his heart, engaging readers with these
witty, passionate, unerring samples of a poet's art. The sonnet! Is there any cash
in it? Its branches grow and grow and are dendritic. Just touch these suns. Scorn
not the sonnet, Critic.

The formalist couldn't "hear" the sonnet. He *argued* with me that it wasn't a sonnet and that the only rhymes he heard were "dendritic" and "Critic." Finally, I printed it out for him as a sonnet, and, finally, he saw it. He sent it to his friends as a good joke, as if he had known it all the time.

—I think it's a question of reading with your eyes rather than with your ears— of not really "listening" to the words, which is the way we're taught to read prose: silently. What I did is clearer if you read the passage aloud. Cf. Saint Augustine, Book Six, The Confessions. *Augustine is stunned to see his friend, Ambrose (later, Saint Ambrose), reading silently. What is suddenly clear is that the rise of Christianity and silent reading go hand in hand. "Inwardness."*

How many people, even poets, read with their ears?

*

HIGH PUNDAY MOURN HEN SPRANG
—answering Shelby Wall's "A pun what?" (upon what? a pun, what!)

A pun a miry die win sprang eye tuck high thrust and bury whack. Eye plied hay hairy gritty made hand missed hire pun hair beak.

Upon a merry day in spring I took my customary walk. I spied a very pretty maid and kissed her on her cheek.

*

TRUE HATE

Referring to Maureen Dowd's latest salvo against Donald Trump, my son remarked, "And he cares what she says." I answered, "Yes, he cares, but even more: Most people spend time in identifying their friends; deeply combatant in his nature, he spends tremendous amounts of time in identifying his *enemies*. That's why his alliances slip from him so easily whereas his enmities are forever."

*

SECOND COMING

first coming: sex
second coming: power

*

Chatting with some people at a party. "Jacktalk."
An acquaintance walked up to me and said,
Firmly, with no trace of good humor or irony,
"*I hate you.*"
I turned away from the friends
To whom I had been speaking,
Looked at him, and said,
"*I know,*"
Then turned back to my conversation.
Not knowing what to say,
He hesitated for a moment
And walked away,
Awash with confusion.
—*It was himself*
It was himself
It was himself
That he hated.

*

Words: Why does the word "doubt" have a b in it?
Because it is etymologically related to the word,
"dou*b*le." To doubt something is to feel *two ways*
about it. The "doubts" we feel about Cary Grant
in Hitchcock's *Suspicion*—is he or isn't he a murderer—
are thus related to the many "doubles" we see in
Hitchcock's films: Mrs. Froy in *The Lady Vanishes*,
for instance, or Van Meer in *Foreign Correspondent*.

*

Scorsese? what about stories
dealing with what Indians *are*
rather than with what whites
did to them—Indians as victims?
have you seen or heard of
I Heard the Owl Call My Name
with the great actor, Tom Courtney?
or seen or heard of Kasi Lemmons'
wonderful *Eve's Bayou*? there are
no white people in the film at all. it's
not about black-white relations.
it's about relations within an active
and thriving black community, and
more specifically about a family
within that community. Scorsese
bought into the ultimately racist
notion that you have to have whites
(nasty ones perhaps but whites)
in a film about Native Americans.
(and the whites he uses are very
prominent white actors. *how else*
can you get people to come to the
movie? yet perhaps Scorsese's
name might have been enough, enough
to have made a film about what it's
like to be a Native American NOW.)
Hollywood (and the USA) did to
Indians what they did to Vaudeville:
destroy the institution and then
use the story of its destruction
as interesting subject matter.

*

Astaire, Kelly, Baryshnikov—but have you seen Tommy Rall??

*

QUESTIONABLE BEHAVIOR

I am tempted to write a film script
Called QUESTIONABLE BEHAVIOR.
In this script people would do things
That were legal but unethical.
They would profit at the expense
(Pun intended) of others.
Nor would the questionable
Behavior be limited to the characters.
I should like to point out
That writing a film script Is a prime example of questionable behavior.
Look what it did to F. Scott Fitzgerald.
And not only writing a film but producing one (Think of Harvey Weinstein)
Or directing one
(Think of John Ford, "The only man who could make John Wayne cry,"
Or of Alfred Hitchcock, who was asked by a Concerned doctor, "Are you trying
to KILL
Tippi Hedren?" The answer
Was probably yes.)
Need I go on about the lives of actors?
I mean the successful ones, leaving
Aside the ones who fail or who achieve
(In Jimmy Carter's wonderful phrase) only "limited success."
How many suffer heartbreak or hopeless dependency
On drugs? How many become total drunks
Who were once sensitive, intelligent people?
How many become crazies like Marlon Brando
Or tragic heroines like Marilyn Monroe, Peg Entwhistle, and Jean Spangler?
I know of two
Who murdered their wives
And then themselves.
Better to find
Something else to do,
To stay in the darkness of unfame
In a nice house
With plenty of DVDs
And a pretty girl or boy
Who has strong arms, a great smile,
And talented underwear.

for Mark Fisher

*

—Our regular conductor here in Palm Beach once upon a time was first principal trumpet under Lennie in the NyPhil. He gave me my lessons so you could say I'm the musical progeny of Leonard Bernstein.

—Ah, wait till you start doing Young Peoples Guides…

—Young Peoples Guide to Palm Beach.

—My gawd what happened to that quarter? You palmed it.

—By gad, sir, I did

—Life is a beach.

—Stormy and limitless.

—*Comes the rain and we all disappear.*

—As the Germans say: "Wir sind nicht aus Zucker."

—Wir sind nur Zucker. Welcome, Zucker. Leave your wallet on the bar.

*

RAY (responding to an image of JACK): I believe there's a great poet hiding in that cityscape.
JACK: Nah, I hear he's just a great writer of wrongs. Unlike The Lone Ranger, who is a great righter of wrongs. Or D. Trump, who is a great wronger of rights. (And isn't it true that The Lone Ranger and Tonto come from Hawkeye and Chingachgook in *The Last of the Mohicans*?)

*

Duende
In the dark
In the rain.
Love
"Like the lion's
Tooth."

*

FORMS

The formal "poet"
    THE FORMAL "POET"
entered a little villanelle
    ENTERED A LITTLE VILLANELLE
looking for his sonnet
    LOOKING FOR HIS SONNET
but he stayed to watch
    BUT HE STAYED TO WATCH
a ghazal strip.
    A GHAZAL STRIP.

*

ignoramuses
    ignora-muses

*

BERKELEY, 60'S

it was not difficult to choose:
on one side there were people
who looked like you.
on the other side
there were only
cops.

*

AFTER THE PASSING

now that she is gone,
I think of something
a friend said
about Saint Augustine:
"sometimes you can't tell
if he is talking about
the afterlife in heaven
or the afterlife in a book."
for these early readers
the dream of heaven
and the dream of the book
merged.
I dream as well and wonder
if faith is anything other than
a wish.
may your mother do well
on her difficult journey.
may this passionate reader
find her way
to the Book of Life,
where she is both reader
and the subject
of reading.

for Angela Manly

*

the video
must have been
from the policeman's
camera.
we saw a young woman,
Stephenie,
if I remember
correctly.
she had just

run over
two people
with her car,
killing them.
whatever "I"
within her
could recognize
this fact
was not operative.
she thought of herself
as a good citizen.
she pointed out
to the policeman
that she had phoned
911.
she helped the
policeman
try to give the victims
help.
she was breezy
with the policeman,
told him she was
on her way to Las
Vegas. "You can
drink all you want
there." she failed
the breath test.
she asked
the policeman
when she could
get her car back.
he said, "Your
car was totaled, wrecked."
she said, "How
will I get to school
tomorrow?" "School," the
policeman said,
"You're not going
to school tomorrow, you're
going to jail. You
killed two people
and you can't even
recognize that. *I
think that's
disgusting.*"

she paused, said, "You're
a cop and
you can say that
to me?"
he said, sounding
just like Sergeant Friday,
"Yes, ma'am, I can."
she got 14
years.

*

        —Ed,
        I am haunted
        by your drowned
        face
        which I did not
        see.
        you come to me
        not as you were in life
        but in your last
        moments.
             —for Edward Lewis Pechter, RIP

*

there are times
when we lose
the connection
to our lives,
when we begin
to disbelieve
even in our finest
accomplishments,
times when darkness
places its hold upon us.
a friend phoned this morning.
I read him the opening poem
of my book, *Creative Death*.
I could feel
his reaction to every word,

feel his excitement
as I read
and suddenly,
though I had lost
touch with the poem,
everything about it
came back to me,
I understood again
why I had placed it
at the opening
of the book.
though it was not
his intention
(he was just listening
to a friend's poem),
my friend, Michael C. Ford,
gave me my poem again,
showed me
that morning
when he phoned
all I had forgotten
about a poem I called
"…DESIRE."

*

"Fighter," "will"—these seem to me to be indications of individual force, of ego, whereas the fundamental gesture of I—'s poetry, what allows it to happen at all, is precisely the opposite of that: it is an act of submission, away from individual force, ego, will, to a figure he calls "'that' goddess." It is "her" speech, not "his," that constitutes the poem—an entity that is only partially (at best) under the poet's control. His position is similar to what Robert Graves speaks of in *The White Goddess* or to D.H. Lawrence's "Not I, not I, but the wind that blows through me." Far from being a fighter, I— simply gives up, submits, allows the poem to have its way with him. He doesn't "will" the poem: he "allows" it. That the poem uses I—'s learning, even aspects of his biography is true, but the poem is not finally self-expressive. It arises out of a space that I—— regards as profoundly other: D.H. Lawrence: "Not I, not I, but the wind that blows through me." It isn't a question of "will" but of "inspiration," of "breathing in."
—But no one believes in inspiration anymore!

> (To I—) An incredible spiritual restlessness is at the heart of your work. You are constantly dissatisfied with wherever it is you are.

Is home Mexico? Is home the U.S.? You are doubled not only in your relationship with Joe but in the deep area of the circumstances of your abiding. "You aren't Americans, you're Indians." Your work creates a consciousness—brilliant, resonant, funny, learned—that fundamentally belongs *elsewhere*. "Home" is the place in which that consciousness is functional and alive, but the only actual place in which it is functional and alive is language. "Home" is where you belong but "home" isn't anywhere: it is always a profound absence: "sound, noise that reaches for the ever receding light." I think that, underneath all the "influences," is this deep longing which is always asserted and always denied.

*

"Use the force, Luke."
"Hello, operator, get me the police."
"Not *that* force, Luke."

*

> a book is a memory
> sealed and abandoned
> —and abandoned

*

ASEMIC: Its lure is that it BOTH has and has not meaning. It exists not as meaning but as POSSIBLE meaning. We remain in a state like that of negative capability: we never arrive at any fully realized ground. It is a deep response to our distrust of—and simultaneous desire for—meaning.

*

"In your work the I is always there—dissolving."

*

"Poetry soothes
and emboldens
the soul
to accept
mystery."
    —Keats

*

"The book
almost finished
almost
seems good."
    —Baudelaire

*

"*You must not understand your life,
Then it becomes a feast*"
    —Rilke (my italics)

*

The notion of poetry originating not in the operations of the poet's ego but in the hearing of voices is one that haunts twentieth-century work. Dylan Thomas, walking on a hill hearing the voices of dead women, is more or less equivalent to Pound's hero, Ulysses, descending into Hades and immediately hearing the clamor of voices. And of course the enormously influential poem, T.S. Eliot's "The Waste Land," is a poem of voices. What Pound and Eliot are hearing in these voices is at once a perception of an activity in their own consciousness and a perception of history as voices—the voices of the past. "Mind" here becomes not the operations of the ego—what "I" think—but an awareness of a sonic multiplicity whose unity is constantly in question. *Under Milk Wood* takes its place in works raising exactly that awareness.

*

            Collisions—
            openings

in the dark theater,
an escape
into the light—

(there is no
"subconscious"
he sd,
there is only
mind
in its changing
motions
of known
and unknown:
"revision"
he added,
is addition,
not subtraction)

*

JACK:
They were so sophisticated that they named their dog after a French playwright:
Feydeau.
FACEBOOK FRIEND: Phailledeaux is good....
JACK: Throw him a bon.

...

ANOTHER FACEBOOK FRIEND: Sorry for this loss in your life!
JACK (sighing): After a certain point perhaps, loss *becomes* life.

...

[To love that well which thou must leave ere long?
    Typo?   ...which thee *must leave ere long?]*

...

We men are told (and sometimes say) that men are instructed that they ("big
boys") shouldn't cry. But I don't remember ever being told that, and, to tell the

truth, I have always wept easily—a condition that became even more intense
after Adelle's death, tears always at the edge of my eyes. There is of course the
derogatory term, "crybaby," but the only place I can think of that suggests that a
person ought not to cry is the song, "It's My Party and I'll Cry If I Want To."
But the song is about a girl, not a boy. On the other hand, the song was *written*
by three men: Herb Wiener, John Gluck, Jr., and Wally Gold. It is possible that
men keep the story going because it is popular with those women who, like
Anaïs Nin, are "in favor of the sensitive man." I do remember being accidentally
on stage with Anaïs Nin. Suddenly my eye caught hers, and she stumbled in her
speech. A few moments later, she said in her slightly accented speech, "You
look into someone's eyes and you know all their story."

                              *

                    there is an artist—
                    a wonderful man—
                    who contacted me
                    after a radio
                    broadcast.
                    he didn't speak
                    of himself,
                    though I learned later
                    that he painted,
                    wrote,
                    played music.
                    it was the painting
                    that first convinced
                    me
                    of his brilliance,
                    marvelous, mythic
                    pieces
                    though he was also
                    capable
                    of delicate landscapes,
                    portraits.
                    I didn't think anyone
                    had heard of him.
                    finally, I asked
                    for paintings
                    to adorn my new book
                    and he gave them,
                    gladly.
                    I do not believe

in God, Fate, Destiny,
none of these things,
yet must acknowledge
moments of magic
that come to us
not because we
deserve them
("use every man after his
desert,
and who shall
'scape whipping")
but for no reason
other than
that we are there
and they
are there.
magic roams the world
as we roam the world
and sometimes,
as when I met Adelle,
as when I met Argüelles,
as when I met Sangye,
they intersect.
how many good angels are there
who never know
that they have wings?

*

NO SELF!

the notion of the value
of unity
is linked to the value
of individuality
(by etymology
in-dividuus,
"not divided"):

what is the value
what is the value
of a fruitful
chaos?

*

Heidegger: thinking = thanking

*

In Melville's *Billy Budd*, the three central characters, Captain Vere, Claggart, and Billy, all have limitations to what they can perceive: there are things that lie outside their perception of the world. Vere believes in forms, measured forms but cannot see anything that transcends that notion. "Struck dead by an angel of God. But the angel must hang." Evil Claggart hates the idea of innocence and comes upon its very embodiment in Billy Budd, though in fact, as Melville points out, Billy is indeed fallen: his stutter is proof that "the envious marplot of Eden still has something to do with every human consignment." Nonetheless, Billy is unable to see evil, which is why he can exclaim, "God bless Captain Vere." For him, everything, even his own destruction, is good. The Captain, faced with something outside the limits of his world view—Billy's killing of Claggart—in effect kills Billy so that his world view can survive unchallenged; the same is true of Billy, which is why he kills Claggart. He too cannot stand to see something that contradicts his world view. The only person who can come near to seeing *all* of reality is Herman Melville, but this very ability dooms the author to ambiguity. He is a man at sea, and the sea is human consciousness: "*an unstable republic of conflicting impulses, instincts, and appetites in perpetual flux.*" I had these thoughts in my early twenties and return to them now, return to them now.

*

VON ARMEN B.B.
—from Brecht's German

I, Bertolt Brecht, come from the black forests
My mother brought me to the cities
As I lay in her womb. And the cold of the forests
Will be with me till the day I die.

In the asphaltcities I'm at home. From the very start
Given every last sacrament:
Newspapers, tobacco, brandy.

Mistrustful, lazy, in the end content.

I'm friendly to people. I wear
A stiff hat because that's what they do
I say: They are animals that stink
And I say: It doesn't matter, I'm one too.

In the early hours, I offer a seat
To a couple of women. My rocking chairs are empty.
I look at them steadily and intently, and I say:
"You can't rely on me."

Towards evening I associate with men.
We address each other as "gentlemen."
They have their feet up on my table top
And they say, "Things will get better for us." I don't ask "When?"

In the early morning light the fir trees piss
And their vermin, the birds, begin to scream.
At that hour I finish my drink in the city and toss away
My cigar butt and, uneasily, sleep, dream.

We have sat, an uneasy, light generation
In houses said to be incapable of destruction
(Thus have we built those big boxes on Manhattan Island
 And the thin Antennae that entertain the Atlantic Ocean).

What will remain of these cities? What passed through them, the wind!
The house makes the eater happy: he clears it out.
We know we are only provisional, tenants,
And after us will come: nothing much to talk about.

In the earthquakes to come, I hope
My cigar will not go out because of the bitterness that will grow,
I, Bertolt Brecht, carried to the asphaltcities
From the black forests, in my mother's womb, so long ago.

*

    —it is not generally known
    that Bertolt Brecht
    was a regular feature
    of an American TV show

in the 1950s,
though he was never credited.

back in the 1920s,
before Kurt Weill provided considerably better music,
Brecht sang his lyrics
to his own tunes
in the Berlin cabarets.
Brecht (like Dylan!) was reasonably successful
but Weill improved his tunes immeasurably.
Brecht decided to record
two from *Die Dreigroschenoper*:
"Ballade von der Unzulänglichkeit"
& "Moritat."

he did not sing especially well
and the recordings
are simultaneously wonderful and ludicrous.

for a time
the *Die Dregroschenoper* music
was a feature
of the Nazi
"Museum of Decadent Art"
until it attracted so many people
that it was removed.

the American TV comedian, Ernie Kovacs,
Hungarian, not German,
played Brecht's rendition of "Moritat"
regularly as background on his show.
Kovacs always included
the verse in which Mackie
rapes—for pay—an underaged
widow.
     Und die minderjährige Witwe…

this recording
went out into the Puritan consciousness
of the American 1950s
in which Lucy and Desi,
who everyone knew were actually married,
could not inhabit
the same bed
on their TV show.

I wonder
how many displaced Germans
were in Hollywood or New York in the 1950s?
I wonder:
didn't anyone—did Kovacs?—speak German?

*

FOR WES NISKER: A LITTLE TUNE

goodbye
scoop
jews buddhism
the fucking war
—I knew you a little
ran into you on telegraph
exchanged pleasantries…

.

scoop:
sailors face the terrors
of wind and sea and sky

*

LINDA,

my dentist's
receptionist,
was a sweet,
considerate
person.
everyone agreed
about that.
she knew
about my difficulties
with the many steps
that led to his office.
once,
I arrived to pick up

some tubes
of special tooth paste.
she said, "Don't worry,
I'll bring them down
to you."
she retired
a year or two ago.
they discovered
that the cancer
had spread to her spine.
she had two months
of severe pain
before the cancer,
mercifully,
took her.
now tell me
about a loving,
benevolent
God.

*

I've been writing since I was 15. I think it is the burden of my entire life's work to find ways of balancing (not integrating, balancing) my capacity for knowledge and my capacity for the intuitive, for poetry. I've written poems that are also "reviews" and are labeled as such. One deals with *Streetcar Named Desire.* I believe I'm the first person to describe Stanley Kowalski as "rough trade," so there is an element of analysis and discovery in that sense—but it is a poem as well. I think "rough trade" is also a factor in Emlyn Williams' great play, *Night Must Fall,* and I have written a poem-review of that as well. My sense is that whatever gave birth to us is not omniscient but has an enormous need to know itself. (I get this notion from Bernard Shaw and his "Life Force.") I think that each of us is *an experiment in knowing*, in self-awareness. Humans are the only creatures to have developed this aspect of mentation so fully, whether we speak of art, science, architecture, music, stories, etc. The way to knowledge is through the intuitive, through what we *don't* know. We may arrive at some form of knowledge, but we must then plunge again into the not known, for there is always more. It is not for nothing that the early Christian church made "Curiosity" (the thirst for *knowledge*), a major sin. It is what put Dante's Ulysses in hell.

Considerate la vostra semenza:
fatti non foste a viver come bruti,
ma per seguir virtute e canoscenza.

"Consider the seed from which you sprang:
You were not made to live as beasts,
But to follow virtue and *knowledge*."

[WHATEVER BROUGHT US HERE
WISHES TO KNOW
ITSELF: TO COMPREHEND
ITS OWN
VAST
IS]

listening
to the great
Barber Shop quartet,
The Buffalo Bills
reminds me
that what we call
"the individual"
is not "undivided"
(*in-dividuus*)
but chordal,
resonant.
we are all
the choral cry
of voices
seeking
what *Genesis*
and the early Church
and even Dante
Alighieri
forbid:
knowledge]

*

The appalling
American
Ignorance of grammar began
With my generation. I saw it

Accelerate in teachers when
My son went to school. "Just
Express yourself. Don't
Worry about grammar." My
Generation knew that when
You knocked on a door and
Someone said, "Who is it?"
Your "natural" impulse was to say,
"It's me" (as the French do:
"C'est moi") but that
"It is I" was correct.
Unfortunately,
The notion that "I" was *always*
Correct and "me" incorrect
Got applied all the way
Across the board, despite
The fact that the *only* verb
To which it applied
Was *To Be.*
When Anita Loos published her
Autobiography in 1966, she
Jokingly called it *A Girl Like I.*
I heard Shirley MacLaine
Use exactly that expression
Without a hint of irony or
Amusement
On an American
Television program.
I remembered the teachers
In Sean's first school.
Thou shalt not worry
About grammar.

*

The aliveness that I associated with the intense experience of poetry in 1955
thrust me into a larger world—a world in which the solidity of "I" disappeared
and moved me in various directions. For me it wasn't LSD or Indian philosophy
or any philosophy (though Heidegger had a powerful influence) but a sense of
the infinitude of language that brought me into poetry. I have recently thought of
poetry as words constantly in motion, constantly moving beyond themselves,
whether they appear in the form of verse or prose. Ecstasy seems to be linked to
the instability of language.

*

I turned 83 in August, 2023, and at such an advanced age you begin to gather together what you have done—all the fluttering leaves: this is what expressed itself through me ("Not I, not I, but the wind that blows through me"); may it have been of some value for those who listened. People ask me whether I have ever been an actor. I have never been an actor, have never had ambitions in that direction. I do feel, however, that poets ought to be able to present their poems orally in an effective way. But that doesn't mean that a poet has to be an actor. You are not responding to a "character," a pretend person, not trying to be "someone else." You are responding—intensely—to words.

*

AT THIS TIME WHEN DEMOCRACY IS UNDER ATTACK

do you want to know about democracy
do you want to know what it is
listen to The Mills Brothers and Louis Armstrong
singing Irving Berlin's great songs,
"Marie"
and "The Song is Ended"—
you will hear
harmonious disagreement,
the sudden flare
of Armstrong's magnificent horn,
the dialectic
of the one
and the many
discussed & amplified,
the soft guitar
beneath it all,
the discovery
of a new melody
within the melody
the throb of rhythm
the deep
respect
of all these people
for each other—
the ineluctable, democratic face
of "listening"

*

From a friend:

"This quotation from Thomas Wolfe is an accurate description of you, as well: 'I will go everywhere and see everything. I will meet all the people I can. I will think all the thoughts, feel all the emotions I am able, and I will write, write, write....' When I witness your dynamism, I think of the comment a Yale psychologist made of William Carlos Williams in the *Voices & Visions* video series, 'The man was simply too much.'"

My answer:

Thank you (*I think*!).

The "I will go everywhere" quotation is a wonderful encapsulation of the hunger for experience we feel as adolescents. Jack Kerouac, deeply influenced by Wolfe, paraphrases it in his famous "The only people for me are the mad ones" passage from *On the Road*. Wolfe's awareness of this feeling is one reason why people tend to discover him—as I did—when they are adolescents. Essentially it is an ego hunger, a push forward by the author's I to expand itself. The dreadful film, *Genius*, purportedly about Wolfe's relationship to his editor, Maxwell Perkins, takes egotism to be Wolfe's essential characteristic. He is "a great writer" but it all comes from what's "in his head" so he is more or less a monster of egotism whereas Perkins, though perhaps not a "genius," is an admirable family man, an all-round good fellow.

This view of Wolfe leaves out something important: the fact of the enormous vividness—in what they do, in what they say, and especially in how they say it—of the characters in *Look Homeward, Angel*. Listen to my radio show on Tuesday. Wolfe's wonderful story, "Only the Dead Know Brooklyn," is narrated in full Brooklyn idiom by an unnamed Brooklyn native who encounters (who else?) Thomas Wolfe on the subway. I'm not noted for my powers of mimicry, but all I had to do was pronounce what Wolfe put on the page in order to sound like an authentic dweller in Brooklyn. (People have said to me, "That wasn't *you*.") What Wolfe wrote isn't mockery or exaggeration, which you might get in a lesser writer: it sounds "real." This is not possible via egotism: it is only possible via the opposite of egotism: empathy.

James Joyce's great short story, "The Dead," is a brilliant example of the movement out of egotism into a sense of deep empathy, a sense of kinship with "all the living and the dead." I believe Joyce identifies this movement with the arc the artist has to travel: it is finally what Molly Bloom's soliloquy is all about: "Yes, I said yes, I will, yes." I believe further that this is what animates Thomas Wolfe's work as well. Charles Olson memorably called it "the figure of outward"—a kind of salvation for people most dreadfully caught up in the inwardness and narcissism of "the lonely crowd."

I wrote this in tribute to Joyce:

master,…
words
winged with your consciousness
touch us in the deepest places.
you understood
that the arc
of the artist
was not to express
egotism
but to move
out
from it,
to arrive at a larger vision
than was possible
in ordinary circumstance,
and that the key
to this
movement
was nothing less
than
the upward
flight,
the multilogic
aspect
of
words:
falling faintly, faintly falling

*

FOR SHAJIL ANTHRU
(born Jan 27)

turning again in the whirl
of consciousness
opening myself to the plenitude

in which we swim or drown
listening to the loved
voices that give me news
of being
(echoing Whitman and the "cradle")
this joy of knowing
without knowing
(agnosia)
this bliss
of speech
that is more than
speech—
all this comes to me
as I think of your birth,
my friend
on the other end
of the earth,
we meet
in a seesaw of lovingness
as we recognize
shared longings
magnificent vistas
rich imaginations
of a world
we cannot fully tell
the contours of.
this is what it means
to "redefine the world"
to assert
the limitations of the real
and give imagination
its all-embracing
plenitude

and crown
of thorns.

*

MALBEARERS

"…front door, as
I slammed it, I nearly cut,
all the way off,
the tops of both
first fingers, right
hand, ambulance, surgery…"
we all have,
in our deepest depths,
creatures—malbearers—
who wish us ill.
no one who lives
is without them
& they touch us
when we are most
vulnerable,
after great loss,
or in the midst
of fierce conscious
turbulence:
they tell us
life
isn't worth it,
that we are
damaged goods.
they crouch
in our dark
crevices
& whisper
& try to guide our hands
to harm.
we cannot
hate them,
they
are part of us,
but we can
recognize
their instigations
& know
that in their innocence
they have no knowledge
but destruction
no love

but the obliteration
of whatever lives.
it is known
that they are at their worst
among the best,
the purest of heart.
resist them.
resist them.
are we not—
all of us—
an experiment
in living,
an attempt
to clarify
the very breath
we breathe.

We breathe.

*

ANGELA MANLY/*JACK FOLEY*

It's Autumn,
  Fall,
the eleventh day
  Eleven days
of the waxing moon.
  Since the moon began to grow.
Luminous,
  I think of her elegant
with occasional clouds.
  Fingers as she writes
Like in a Li Bai poem!
  These words!

*

AT THE CROSSROADS:
A BALLAD OF A LIE ABOUT ROBERT JOHNSON

There's a dark man waiting
down by the crossroads
they say he's older
than a thousand years
holds a knife in one hand
in the other a guitar
they say when you meet him
you flow with tears
I'll see, I'll see

He's got a million names
but one's old nick
seen a million things
go down the stream
he'll never be blessed
but he'll never die
I always thought
he was just a dream
I'll see, I'll see

my name is Robert
son of John
I want my hands
to learn to play
he says I have
an immortal soul
if I have it's his
I'm in his sway
I'll see, I'll see

Dear Robert, Dear Robert
says my soul to me
Dear Robert, Dear Robert
you still are free
you still can refuse
his foul commands
music comes pouring
from my willing hands
I'll see, I'll see

CHIP DEFAA'S CD, *THE GEORGE M. COHAN SONGBOOK*

give my regards to broadway
harrigan
I've seen them all
I'm going to fall
for a small
town girl
        never such innocence
my mother's name
was Mary
down by the Erie Canal
goodbye, Flo
        never such innocence again
give my regards to broadway
play it slowly
and it's mournful
play it quickly and it's
full of energy and hope.
isn't that an Irish thing?
so long, Mary—
this reminds me of my family
on the day I left Schenectady
to the depot then they came
with me
I even hear them say…
        never such innocence
        never such tenderness
        matched with a knowing
        air
only 45 minutes from
not a saloon in the
it's the same old song they sing:
I love you
        what longing in the man
the Nell of all Nellies
        (his mother's name)
these wonderful songs
touch a place in me
that was formed
when I was a child and heard them.
I hear some in my father's voice
some in the voices of these
wonderful singers.
in the fine film,
Tous les Matins du Monde,
someone says

that the point of music
is to raise the dead.
I feel that spirit here,
feel the presence
of a complex man
who lived in the imagination
of all he failed to have
as a child,
the towns he played
but didn't live in,
and of the sweet care he felt
from the loving
family
that was his
anchor
and his world

*

o tater fraterabo
no stasis in poesis
o static attic exodus
whose cases are these cases?
o fraterabo tater
do thy mater and thy pater
know that either soon or later
the grim EXTERMINATOR
will cause thee endless woe?
no?
Ah, tater fraterabo!
Ah, fraterabo tater!
Ave atque Wally…

*

last night
Sangye and I
watched
South Pacific.
Ezio Pinza

would have been
in the film
but he died
so they hired
an Italian actor
who couldn't sing
(this despite the fact
that the character
was supposed to be
French, not Italian:
these were the days
of Renzo Cesana,
"The Continental":
"ah, welcome, dear lady…").
in this film
practically everyone,
including Juanita Hall,
was dubbed.
I never saw *South Pacific*
but I had seen Pinza
in *Fanny*, a brilliant
but more or less forgotten
Broadway musical:
he was marvelous.
he was not the lead
but an unforgettable presence
when he sang a few bars
of the beautiful title song.
as I watched
Rossano Brazzi
mouthing the sounds
of the singer Giorgio Tozzi
I began to imagine
what Pinza must have been like
when he stepped to the footlights
and in that magnificent *basso*
sang "Some Enchanted Evening."
who had heard such a voice
in any musical?
I began to weep his absence
from the film,
death's hand upon him.
Sangye saw my weeping
and putting a loving hand
on my arm,

she said sweetly, not cruelly,
"Softie."
I said, "I know."

*

"The reward of the young scientist is the emotional thrill of being the first
person in the history of the world to see something or understand something.
Nothing can compare with that experience…The reward of the old scientist is
the sense of having seen a vague sketch grow into a masterly landscape."
    —Cecilia Payne-Gaposchkin, astronomer

   …

—*I believe that the experience of "creativity" is far less the experience of "self-
expression" than it is the experience of a sense of being "the first person in the
history of the world to see something or understand something." Dylan Thomas
says it's like "seeing eggs laid by tigers." And Payne-Gaposchkin is right:
"Nothing can compare with such an experience." It takes hold like a drug. I am
of course speaking of a feeling, not of a "fact." What the feeling expresses may
not be "true": it is only a feeling, but the excitement it generates is amazing. It
takes hold like a drug. Think of Keats: he must have believed that no one,
absolutely no one had ever thought that beauty and truth were identical until
that thought came to him. "Then felt I like some watcher of the skies / When a
new planet swims into his ken." "A masterly landscape."*

*

LETTERS

thr gsbot bivyim yhr derryinhd yhr nounfsty
yhr dvugg
yo slloe yhr dprvisllplainted grass bag
refuse to divulge
yhr eoetlf ot yr nrst nr vsllrf yo sloe yhr dpitiyd yhodr mrfis
I eill trvkon him
yhr rdyrrm in ehivh nre yrttioyyt
ehivh oyhrtd msy ginf yoo Vhtidyisn
the likelihood that the village

you ertr s punliv return had no connection sll in bsin
motr onr yhsn snoyhrt brty yhivk zz & Isthr
we talked of a part of the craving the fullest satisfact ion
errk dytryvh
I hsbr likrnrf you yhr noyr og s honh   *when he kills*
in new territory
in domr indysnvrd yhr nrst id pryiyionrf
            fur yo hhr dhspinh hsnf & yhr philodophivsl minf
to allow the spirits
iy id ptimstily sd s vtiyiv eiyh Johndon I quarrle
plrsde etiyr.   Snf iy eill trsvh mr.
Yhsy duvh udrd dhoulf hsbr rcidyrf eiyh duvh trginrmrny
hr fif noy hrdiysyr sd yo yhr voutdr ihr esd yo putdur
the dpsnidh volonisl hidyoty
to hold to this communivsion
nsvk yo yhr brddrld
yhr duvvrddion esd vonyrnyrf
yhr glrry hrlf iyd voutdr
yhr golloeinh motninh
yhr mrn eotr s doty og s msnyir
ig you trgudr yhry vonvlufrf imiysiond yhr dyshr in ehivh
            for greater mortifications
likened to the note of a gong has survived however noble
yhr life of las cases hs been several times written
pudhrf on yhtrr 2o to5u 14wyu4e
llrlivi llrlfo
snoyhrt ysnk vondidyrf on s gull lion
vuy in yhr dolif tovk
            my bslusyiond og poryd hsbr trmsinrf ptryy vondysny

gnbie
ciooobppwrewqqqq
qetwxtycsf
ahhhhhhhhhhhhhhhhhhhhh

            dedicated to the sixth Marx Brother, Typo

*

            (a friend
            a visual artist
            tells me

he is going
blind
I can barely tell you
the sorrow
and bewilderment
he/I must feel—
When I consider how my light is spent....)

*

In its initial impulses, Surrealism was an attempt to liberate the mind
through the violent juxtaposition of oppositions; it arose out of a
situation shot through with contradictions and was vehemently *against*
any attempts to mediate among those contradictions. As such,
Surrealism moved away from any affirmation of "ego" or "unity." It
was an announcement, in the loudest possible terms, of utter chaos—"a
bomb," as Max Ernst called Dada. By contrast, in many popular current
poets "Surrealism" is an assertion of the author's admirably "poetic"
sensibility; it is, precisely, an *affirmation* of ego: "When *I* lost hearing,
I began to see voices."

*

THE GODHEAD

Shall we give thanks
Shall we offer up
Devotion
To what strangeness
To what otherness
That we strive to
See in our own image
But which cannot be,
Will not be
Grasped. What richness
What poverty
What love
What hatred.
Malkovich to Orlok
In *Shadow of the Vampire*:
"You shall not eat
The members
Of my company!"

*

CLOSE UP

binge-watching
The Twilight Zone
and
Alfred Hitchcock Presents
one notices
certain things
that might be missed
if the programs were seen
only on a weekly
basis.
one is the horrible
fates
of some of the actors:
Gig Young
who was wonderful
in *The Twilight Zone*'s
"Walking Distance,"
murdered his wife
and then himself
in 1978.
so did Albert Salmi
in 1990.
he was memorable
in "The Dangerous People"
on *Alfred Hitchcock Presents*
and in many other programs.
and Kenneth Haigh
who was brilliant
as Jimmy
in the original production
of *Look Back in Anger* (1956)
and excellent in *The
Twilight Zone*'s
"The Last Flight" (1960).
I wondered who he was,
what had happened to him.
he swallowed a bone
in a Soho restaurant

in 2003.
oxygen deprivation
led to brain damage—
he died fifteen years later
in a nursing home.
another thing is the
extraordinary
prevalence
of close-ups
in these films—
far more than
in films made
for theaters:
I think the ruling belief
must have been that television
was a more
intimate medium
than film
and so we needed
to see the actors
close up.
close up
they are.
I remember reading
that when D.W. Griffith,
an early
practitioner,
was told
that audiences
wanted the full figure
of the actors
as in the theater
and not the close up,
he said, *You're looking at me.*
What do you see?
what do *I* see
as I look
at these ancient
films
and think
of the vivid, dying actors—
some murderers,
almost all
dead now?
what do I think

of the striving
of their lives?

*

       "…but the comedy
       of our lives
       must end"

*

SONG

who made those eyebrows   IN MEMORY'S
white   STRANGE
      COUNTRY
who made what hair remains   WHERE WHAT IS
gray   NOT
      IS,
who placed that claddagh   SO MANY
round the neck   SPIRITS
      GREET
do those eyes (my eyes)   YOU,
still see   SMILING

*

NIGHT MUST FALL
    a review

the great
1937
version
with a terrific
performance
by Robert Montgomery
and excellent support

from Rosalind Russell
(intelligence and
repression
personified)
and Dame May Whitty
(how little we care
when he murders her
even as she is saying,
"Dear Danny":
she loves him
even as he murders her)
both women
love him
for what he is
but even more
for what
he is not.
the author of the play
was a gay man
so we are perhaps dealing,
as in *A Streetcar Named Desire,*
with "rough trade,"
with what Oscar Wilde called
"feasting with tigers."
how often our choices
are determined
not by what we want
but what we want
not
to be.
how often our loves
reach for the forbidden
not because it is forbidden
but because it is not
what is near.
the lure of the dark,
of "night."
Gate gate pāragate pārasaṃgate bodhi svāhā.
Going, going, always going beyond.
there is, said Michael McClure,
restlessness
and only
restlessness.
we are rivers
looking for the sea.

*

MEMORY

Sangye & I
Watched the original
(1947)
Miracle on 34th Street,
An excellent
Film,
Beautifully directed
And with excellent
Performances from
Everyone,
Including Natalie
Wood as a child
Actress. (She
Had a photographic
Memory and would
Correct people when
They missed a line.)
I had seen the film
Before, but
It was many, many
Years ago.
I have a distinct
Memory of Edmund
Gwenn as Kris Kringle
Standing in the midst
Of all these people
Arguing whether
He is the real
Santa Claus.
Suddenly,
In the midst
Of all that
Clamor,
He simply
Disappears,
Vanishes—
Proving
He is the real

Santa Claus.
But the scene
Is nowhere
In the film,
Nor in descriptions
Of the film's
Plot.
Did I dream it?
I don't know.
And Natalie
Wood,
No longer a child
In *Rebel Without*
A Cause,
And the insoluble mystery
Of her dark,
Dark
Death.

*

"…of BROADWAY"

in the great
Al Dubin-Harry Warren
song,
"Lullaby of Broadway"
(1935—
the middle
of the Great
Depression),
Broadway
is not Cohan's
longed-for
1906
home ground
("whisper of how I'm
yearning")
but a place
that turns everything
upside down.

it is a lullaby
but the lullaby is anything
but gentle: it
is intense, compelling,
polyrhythmic,
it is insistent that we
MOVE:
it puts us to sleep
not by gently lulling us
but by wearing us out:
you rock-a-bye your baby round
till everything gets hazy.
and the baby named
in this lullaby
is not an infant
but a full-grown
voluptuous
woman—
what the lyric calls
a "daffy-dill,"
Broadway slang
for chorus girls.
there is a "daddy"
who sings this
lullaby
but he is hardly the parent
of the baby:
he is a *sugar* daddy
who tells her,
as one would
tell a child,
"Hush-a bye, I'll
buy you this and that."
furthermore, this baby
has no crib:
she has a "*flat*"
to which she returns
in the morning,
when the *milkman*—
not the sandman—
is *on his way.*
it is a world
in which
everyone
goes crazy.

a world
of *hip hooray*
and bally hoo,
tremendously
exciting,
tremendously
active,
and in the midst
of the great
DEPRESSION
joyful
and
rich.
the entire city
of New York
becomes
a Busby
Berkeley
production
number.
it is a
vision,
an amazement,
the "there"
of Baudelaire's
longing
for an idealized
Holland,
minus the *calme*
but with the *luxe*
and *volupté*.
it summons us
to awaken
even as it tells us
that we will sleep,
sleep, sleep.
it is there
in its innocence
in the dream house
of the movies
four years
before the wizard
who is no wizard
gives us
our hearts,

our brains,
and our longed-for
courage.
it is magic
and desire.
it is also
in this deeply Protestant country
that was, in 1935, deeply in need,
the secular Promise
of the Promised
Land,
the demotic
chiaroscuro
of the heavenly place.
give us this *night*
our daily song.
you've listened to
the lullaby
of old
Broad
Way.

*

collisions, uncertainties, not truths but only possibilities

*

PRENDS PITIÉ…

O Dieu qui n'existe pas
Dieu des choses imaginaires
I invoke thine aid
To adolescent poets
Whose rhymes reflect
Hormonal changes only,
To poets who collect

Rejection slips
And eventually give up,
To good poets whose work
Is never or only partially
Acknowledged,
To all the dark ones
Who slip through the cracks
Of poetic glory
Producers of doggerel
Or bad rhymes
Or of work no one understands
(Or is ever likely to understand)
To those who light a candle
That immediately goes out
And offers no illumination
Have mercy upon them
The talentless
The ignorant
The talented but ignored
All those who ply a thankless trade
All those whose souls
Are bared to no purpose whatsoever
And who suffer
The agonies of revision
To no avail—
Give them dreams
The Enoch Soames's
Of our day,
God who is not only,
Like all gods,
Invisible
But actually
Non-existent,
Nothing but air, thought, desire,
The careless error
Of the longing heart,
Dieu qui n'existe pas
Dieu des choses imaginaires

*

All these lines
which perhaps lead nowhere
came forth
in furious insistence
as I think
of the actual
death of friends
and of the possible
death of friends
and of my own
death
and my wish
to somehow
establish myself
on this
whirling earth
to say
to the dark man
who comes for me
"I lived"

*

*tous les poètes
sont orphée
son histoire
est l'histoire de tous*

*la femme
et sa perte
la descente
dans les enfers*

*la conscience
que la femme
est un aspect
de lui même*
.

*et la musique
toujours, toujours ça*

*

flaught—
a flake

flight

*

                    (singing)
                    toutes mes foutaises
                    toutes mes foutaises
                    me donnent
                    plaisir

*

READING

from time to time
one discovers a book
that has both authority
and an almost magical
command of one's attention.
Robert Lamberton's
Homer the Theologian,
which I have just begun
to read,
seems to be such a book.
it is about "a single phase of the history
of the interaction of the Homeric poems
with Greek ideas concerning
the nature of reality
and the divine: the
reading of Homer by thinkers
in the Platonic tradition
from the second to the fifth century
after Christ."
few readers realize
that when Yeats writes,

"Homer is my example
and his unchristened heart,"
the Homer to which he refers
is not the Homer of Richmond Lattimore—
still less the Homer of Alexander Pope—
but the Homer of that third-century Greek
philosopher, learnéd, vehement opponent
of Christianity, named for the
purple of kings—
Porphyry, author of the once famous
essay on "the cave of the nymphs episode"
in *The Odyssey.* William Blake,
writes Lamberton,
"painted a representation
of the Ithacan cave
based manifestly on Porphyry
rather than Homer."
the allegorical interpretations
of such Neoplatonists
had their effects
on Christian
interpretations
of the Bible,
on what we believe we know
about our official religion.
Homer was *poet*
but the term *theologian,*
usually used of Orpheus,
was now used of him as well.
what changed
was the *reading*
of a text.
I had forgotten
why I *read,*
why *reading*
was important.
we read
for entertainment
for distraction
for instruction
but we also read
(and write)
to allow the words
to fly into our minds
and seek the dark, unlettered places

that long for life and freedom
and are gathered
by words'
        wings.

*

I see the night—the restless, eager night
That spreads its shadow softly on the day,
And whispers to the sun's red, burning light
To vanish like a dream and pass away.

I see the night—the darkened mist of night—
And feel the velvet sorrows mem'ries bring;
September's leaves have fallen, old and bright,
And autumn's winds have blown the dust of spring.

I think of days long past, and gone, and dead,
Of all the ancient, withered hopes I've had,
And wonder where the passing hours have fled—
The ghosts of yesterday—forever sad.

O ghosts, my dreams, once breathing, once alive,
Like flower petals in a hurricane,
Were sundered from their stems, no more to thrive,
No more to feel the gentle touch of rain,

No more to hear my reckless, youthful calls,
But banished into bleak eternity,
To come again to me when darkness falls,
As waves upon the seas of memory.

And now the night, with stars and shining lights
All winking, sprightly, like the woodland fawns,
Is fading fast, for with a thousand nights,
There comes the brilliance of a thousand dawns.

First poem, 1955

*

"[Writing] is always at odds with itself...never achieves what it expects of itself. Constantly it approaches a silence, which can be inherent in extreme violence. It is the violence of non-sense or that of an insignificance that can hardly be mastered. Everyone who writes experiences himself as driven and inhibited by this violence. The insistence on such a language at the edge of language is attributed to the ideology of modernity. But it has always existed. It can be found in Homer and Pindar, in Dante and Shakespeare. There is no writing that is not haunted and inspired by its impossibility."

"'The chaos is the holy itself,' Heidegger writes in his 'Explanations of Hölderlin's Poetry.' What is he...about? One answer could be: to identify what undermines him a priori as a background of logo culture."

—Marcus Steinweg

*

TURNING AND TURNING, AND TURNING

darling,
many of William Butler Yeats' lines
change their meaning
once we allow
for the presence of the
3rd-century Neoplatonist
Porphyry
and other esoteric
elements.
do you remember
"The Second Coming"?
the entire opening passage,
"Turning and turning in the widening gyre
The falcon cannot hear the falconer,"
etc.,
is taken to mean the same thing:
"Mere anarchy is loosed upon the world."
but we have read
Porphyry
and his once-famous essay
on the cave of the nymphs passage
in *The Odyssey*.

Yeats quotes from that essay
extensively
and refers to it
throughout his career.
do you remember?
Porphyry tells us
of two gates:
the gate of generation
and the gate of ascent
to the realm of the gods.
the gates are not separate:
where the one gate is
the other gate is as well.
now, look at the famous
ending of the poem:
"And what rough beast, its hour come round at last,
Slouches towards Bethlehem to be born?"
Bethlehem: that must be the gate of generation.
where is the other gate?
"Turning and turning in the widening gyre
The falcon cannot hear the falconer."
it is strange
after all these years
and all the interpretations of those lines
to discover, as I did one day,
as I sat meditating in a small room,
that the lines did not refer to anarchy.
the falcon is *removing itself* from a world
which is falling apart.
the falconer
is attempting to bring the bird-soul
back to an unlivable
earth
and to the command
of a creature—himself—
who may well have welcomed the beast.
the bird-soul is moving *up*,
towards heaven.
sitting reading,
I suddenly knew
that the bird
was in ecstasy.
it was not an image of anarchy:
it was an image of escape.
darling,

I can't tell you the joy
that realization brought me
along with the stunning
awareness
of how wrong
generations of critics
might be.
I knew
I had a secret
I could tell
and I knew as well
that many
would wish the secret
to stay
secret.
darling,
you see the state
of the man
you love.

for Sangye, who is also Anaïs

END: COLLISIONS

BEOWULF

Master,
The claw of the sea takes the flaming boat
Mother sea   keeps the ashes
Brief fire   (flares and is over)

[JOHN DONNE]
(writing between the lines)
for Iván Argüelles

white side under goes
      who are all these Buddhists?
bleached blank the frame
      no man is.
music in its 17th century
      in the rectory standeth
resounds its unsounded Note
      the lewd don,
to name such things to sleep
      Donne
in the beneath whorled leaf
      Alight
sundered from the starry throng
      in Seventeenth-Century
mind's single core relents
      clear sunnelight
wake then Thou! worm devour
      Dayseye
heart's restless entity alive
      shines in the heart
in search of what underbrush
      Un-
turn each blade around its green
      Donne

link to nerve its everyness
       Lord, Thou singest
the holiday of aching dolorous
       (eye of bone)
will we pine then in the hostel
       Lord, Thou singest
wearing each other's wretched
       Flaming
skin a mask of flame and dross
       Sword's words!
the smoking cadaver in your eye
       Start with stars
will it not wait for the avenue
       Then (all) is donne
with what tense invoke the Holy
       Light is shee
being and its unexplained event
       whose grave (*a bracelet of bright haire!*)
such is hush the eventide
       hath kisses
its instrument yet now dulled
       placed thereon
why the glass in its bleeding
       Shee weeps thy—
light why the merry-go-round
       "Death, be not—"
its painted tigers whirling
       No man is an I
in the eccentric lamp of time
       Nor woman neither
do sit then Soul and nod off
       Stand stille
reckon as no more the day
       and I will read
when thought creates its Air
       This is the shadow
move then around Love's pyre
       This is the deepest shadow
and sitting for the hour whole
       John Donne
divine which is the entrance
       Anne Donne
and which the exit of Paradise
       Undone

　　　　Original poem, "[John Donne]," by Iván Argüelles. Every second line is by me: writing between the lines.

NATA, NATA

in memory of the photographer, Nata Piaskowski

not brooding but some
activity of mind
behind
your smile:
your small size
(always looking up!)
your large eyes
not inquisitive
but demanding
your old-world elegance
your awkwardness
"So how *are* you?" you asked
greeting a friend at the door
in your pleasant, deliberate English
He answered grandly, gesturing with his hands,
"Flourishing"
you didn't understand
hesitated
and asked again
he answered, with the same gesture
and the same smile,
"*Flourishing*"
still not understanding,
you ushered him in
I saw that hesitation

often
you wished the world
to go smoothly
to proceed with the grace you imagined
to be part of your *vie bohème*
and yet
things happened
things you couldn't control or account for:
flourishing
And Martin Baer
dead these many years
Where is the painting he made
of you with the little girl face?
"I know I don't look like that any more,"
you said sadly
If I remember,
there was lots of blue in that painting—
for the virgin Martin saw in you?
Tiny Nata,
everyone towering over you
("She's *mad*," said Josephine Carson, "absolutely *mad*").
"Martin Baer—everyone's *least* favorite painter,"
said Jo,
"even if he *did* look like Jean Cocteau"
I heard him praised by his friend, Robert Duncan
Measured phrases that brought him vividly to life
What a wonderful picture you took of Duncan in his prime!
And how sad you were when you thought he had forgotten you:
"You can't expect everyone to love you always"
But we all expect that, Nata
you no less than anyone else
we all expect love
and moan about sorrow
but you were quiet about your bad luck when you had it
or at least you were to me
I see you seated at that table
(the one in the photo with the rose)
serving me tea
and I suddenly realize: *That's the table in the picture*
Yes, you said, happy about my realization
I felt at times that you evaded intimacy
despite your dinners and lunches
and the young women who loved you and came to learn from you
How you wanted a "set"
something left over from Europe

a group of intimates
who spoke of art and laughed and made you feel free
Now, Nata, you *are* free
of even the visual which was your primary sense
free of all the images that crowded around you
and dominated you and haunted you
in your darkrooms in your long journey from Europe to the New World in
your small light-capturing apartments in your heavy tears in your long long
life in your deep longing in your Polish words that sometimes caused you to
make malapropisms in your home for the aged (where I could not bring myself
to visit you) in your bafflement and strange wonder before the world "I will
take photographs from *my* height I will not stand on a stool" in your dear life
to which you clung with such persistence in your death in your death in your
death

Note: Photographer Nata Piaskowski died at the age of 92. I had known her for
many years. Her photograph of Robert Duncan on the cover of *Bending the
Bow* is a wonder.

THE McCLURIAD

Octogenarian?
The word seems scarcely applicable to the man I see
sitting across the table
of this El Cerrito eatery.

Magnanimous
Inquisitive
Challenging
Happy
Amorous
Elegant
Laughing

"Writhing multidimensionality of thought" *
"The surge of life drifts in every direction."
"I think all art should be extreme."

"Demands for communication are of small voice when art is pushing towards a oneness with the possibilities of imagination."

"EACH. EACH SIDE OF EACH DUST SPECK
turning in sunlight is a movie.
C
A
V
E
S
in the movies
reach to the tiny end of infinity
and each speck grows
to fill all."

"If the type and placements of lines seem strange, read them aloud
and they will take their shape"

MANJUSHRI
Comedian
Clairvoyant
Lover
Ursine (California variety)
Radiant
Energy

"seated on his white lion,
swinging the sword
of
CONSCIOUSNESS
into deeper mines
than our knowing"

"a self portrait without a mirror"

Here is a perfect melting and merging of all realms, the all-in-one and the one-in-all, the dissolving of being and non-being, the convergence of Voidness and existence...All these mysteries of totality consist...in one basic principle: namely, all things...are void. In contrast to doctrines of various monisms and monotheisms, the Hwa Yen Doctrine holds that the wonders of Dharmadh tu are brought into play not because of the one, but because of the great Void. This is as if to say that zero, not one, is the foundation of all numbers.

the mutual penetration and Non-Obstruction of realms **

"Would a sensitive man of Periclean Greece taken up from time and placed in the N.Y.C. Garment Center at rush hour, or in Peking, or Tokyo, or London, imagine himself in Hell?"

In the act of play, and under the influence of the rebellious imagination, *even war transforms itself*

"the simultaneous expression of spirit and matter."

AGNOSIA
knowing through not knowing

"Perhaps blackness is the best window"

"a full measure of black wine"

But now you put a question to me asking, How shall I think about [God], and what is He? And to this I can only answer you, I do not know ***

"I sensed that [Antonin] Artaud's poetry, a breakthrough incarnate, was a way into the open field of poetry and into the open shape of verse and into the physicality of thought."

Not symbolize but simple eyes

"Sculptured hands
of a seated figure.
Half-closed eyes.
Plain as disturbance and straw
and Grandpa's tin snuff box."

"thoughts
in
the
hands
make
one
big
zero"

"The experience of self is what

all things seek
because it is the deeper breath
they breathe"

"the mind
in a mirror of flames"

--

His mater is delectable,
Solacious, and commendable;
His English well allowed,
So as it is emprowed,
For as it is employed,
There is this mighty Void,
At these dayes moch commended,
O Godde, would men have amended
His English, and do they barke,
And mar all they warke?
McClure, that famus clerke,
His termes were not darke,
But plesaunt, easy, and plaine;
No worde he wrote in vaine.

surge blackness meat SWIRL gesture kid
grahhr

.

There are certain words that are forever
Michael McClure.

■■■■■■■■■■■■■■■■■■■■■■■■■■■■■■■■■■■■■

1955/2013:
Writing between the lines of McClure's poem about the whales

Hung midsea
Not Death,
Like a boat mid-air

Birth
The liners boiled their pastures:
At the poetry reading,
The liners of flesh,
beautiful white hair
The Arctic steamers
streaming,

Brains the size of a teacup
brain sizzling,
Mouths the size of a door
mouthing

The sleek wolves
the vowels and consonants
Mowers and reapers of sea kine.
of Ecstasy.
THE GIANT TADPOLES
Sweet meat,
(Meat their algae)
Ecstatic mammal
Lept
leaps
Like sheep or children
like a child or William Blake
Shot from the sea's bore.
into the fantastical, deep azure of poetic consciousness,
Turned and twisted
turning
(Goya!!)
(Mallarmé!!)
Flung blood and sperm.
blood, bone and sinew
Incense.
into the precise
Gnashed at their tails and brothers
contemplation of air.
Cursed Christ of mammals,
Dionysus
Snapped at the sun,
drunk with the sun,
Ran for the Sea's floor.
Door opener.

Goya! Goya!

Shelley!
Oh Lawrence
Lawrence
No angels dance those bridges.
of the birds, beasts and flowers,
OH GUN! OH BOW!
Angelic presence.
There are no churches in the waves,
There is no church but this,
No holiness,
no holiness,
No passages or crossings
no "passages"
From the beasts' wet shore.
but this man's deep words in the crowded room.

NOTES

* All matter in quotation marks by Michael McClure. The passage in Middle English is an adaptation of a passage by John Skelton in praise of Geoffrey Chaucer.
** Garma C.C. Chang, *The Buddhist Teaching of Totality*—one of McClure's favorite books.
*** *The Cloud of Unknowing.*

ROBERT DUNCAN

master,...
born in Oakland in the depths
of the year (Dec. 7)...
words
winged with your consciousness
touch us in the deepest places.
you understood
that the arc
of the artist
was not to express
egotism
but to move
out

from it,
to arrive at a larger vision
than was possible
in ordinary circumstance
and that the key
to this
movement
was nothing less
than
the upward
flight,
the multilogic
of
words:
My mother would be a falconress,
And I, her gay falcon treading her wrist,
would fly to bring back
from the blue of the sky to her, bleeding, a prize....
McClure told me
you and Jess, with Rexroth,
taught him and the others
how to live
as a poet.
Jess, after your death: *"I can still see Robert*
coming here
from the next
room."

BAUDELAIRE: LA BEAUTÉ

Je suis belle, ô mortels! comme un rêve de pierre,
Et mon sein, où chacun s'est meurtri tour à tour,
Est fait pour inspirer au poète un amour
Eternel et muet ainsi que la matière.

Je trône dans l'azur comme un sphinx incompris;
J'unis un coeur de neige à la blancheur des cygnes;
Je hais le mouvement qui déplace les lignes,
Et jamais je ne pleure et jamais je ne ris.

Les poètes, devant mes grandes attitudes,
Que j'ai l'air d'emprunter aux plus fiers monuments,
Consumeront leurs jours en d'austères études;

Car j'ai, pour fasciner ces dociles amants,
De purs miroirs qui font toutes choses plus belles:
Mes yeux, mes larges yeux aux clartés éternelles!

HOMOPHONIC:

I'm a bell, O mortals, I'm a river named Pierre
And my scene, oooo Jack, you'll get murdered on the tour
He's fay, poor inspirer, who's the poet on the moor?
Eternal deaf mute antsy K's the matty air.

I got thrown in the Azur like a sphinx in capris;
Looney, my cur, bit his pants full of signs
I hate movement, fill the place with fines
And Jimmy J will wear them and Jimmy J will rise.

Poets, diving into their grand platitudes
Which I fear pronto will be fierce monuments,
Consume their tours with these austere studs;

Car J, fascinate these docile ants;
Pure mirrors are a font of frozen cow bells
My use, my large use, is a charity diurnal.

...

LITERAL:

I'm beautiful, mortals, like a dream of stone,
And my sweet breast, where each must pass away,
Inspires in the poets, one by one,
A love eternal and as mute as clay.

Enthroned in Azure, like a sphinx of enigmas—
My heart is snow—to the swan's sheer whiteness keeps,
Hate movement, where dull lines amass;
And so I never laugh and so I never weep.

Poets before my haughty attitudes
(Which evidently come from proudest monuments)

Wear out their days in somber, studious moods

I have, to keep those docile lovers bent,
My eyes, my large bright eyes—pure mirrors turning
All to beauty—my eternal, luminous eyes—they're burning!

…

Oh Death old captain it is time weigh anchor
This country bores us, Death—set sail
If the sky and the sea are black as night
You know our hearts are full of light!

Pour out your poison so it comforts us
This fire burns our brains anew—
                    we want we want
To plunge into the depths of the waters—heaven or hell who cares
In the depths of the unknown to find something new

BAUDELAIRE: INVITATION TO THE VOYAGE

Mon enfant, ma soeur,
Songe à la douceur
D'aller là-bas vivre ensemble!
Aimer à loisir,
Aimer et mourir
Au pays qui te ressemble!
Les soleils mouillés
De ces ciels brouillés
Pour mon esprit ont les charmes
Si mystérieux
De tes traîtres yeux,
Brillant à travers leurs larmes.

Là, tout n'est qu'ordre et beauté,
Luxe, calme et volupté.

Des meubles luisants,
Polis par les ans,
Décoreraient notre chambre;
Les plus rares fleurs
Mêlant leurs odeurs
Aux vagues senteurs de l'ambre,
Les riches plafonds,

Les miroirs profonds,
La splendeur orientale,
Tout y parlerait
À l'âme en secret
Sa douce langue natale.

Là, tout n'est qu'ordre et beauté,
Luxe, calme et volupté.

Vois sur ces canaux
Dormir ces vaisseaux
Dont l'humeur est vagabonde;
C'est pour assouvir
Ton moindre désir
Qu'ils viennent du bout du monde.
— Les soleils couchants
Revêtent les champs,
Les canaux, la ville entière,
D'hyacinthe et d'or;
Le monde s'endort
Dans une chaude lumière.

Là, tout n'est qu'ordre et beauté,
Luxe, calme et volupté.
...

My child my sis-
ter, dream of the bliss
To go down there, we two
To love at leisure
To love and expire
In the country that looks like you.
The wet suns
Of these quarrelsome skies
For me have a charm that nears
The mysteries
Of your vicious eyes
Shining across their tears.

There, nothing but order, beauty—the measure
Of luxury, calm, and sweetest pleasure.

Furniture there
Polished by years
Would decorate our chamber

Rarest flowers
Mixing their scents
With the vague scent of amber
Rich ceilings
Deep mirrors
Oriental splendor
All would speak
To the soul in secret
Its sweet native language.

There, nothing but order, beauty—the measure
Of luxury, calm and sweetest pleasure.

Look at the deep
Canals where they sleep,
These ships that are vagabonds
It is to serve
Your least desire
That they come from the vast world's end
—The suns go to bed
And reclothe the fields
The canals, the entire city
With hyacinth and gold
The world will hold (*Fall*)
(*Asleep*) Itself in a warm shining.

There, nothing but order, beauty—the measure
Of luxury, calm, and sweetest pleasure

W.B.Y.

Gone at 73,
Poet of Ireland
Poet of the Other World
Looking for its traces
In the Wind
Among the Reeds
None like him
For the passion
Of renunciation
"O what a sweetness strayed

To barren Thebaid"
"The foul rag and bone shop
Of the heart"—
Three books
Quote that line
And leave "foul" out—
None like him
For the continual
Recognition
That language
Always goes beyond itself—
Innisfree
Haunted by the words
Of a 3rd-century Neo Platonist—
The immense distance between
This world
And that other
From which
The "voices" came.
Love of the woman
Love of the woman as symbol
The tragedy
That spirit
Lodges itself
In the mire
Of flesh
And that a woman
Must grow old—
Not "unity"
But the fierce knowledge
That all we have
Is the power to know
What we cannot be or emulate.
The swans
Leap up in the pool
And descend again, and leap again.
I love him for the clarity of his monumental, daring, unerring vision.

.

I have lived with him throughout my life
Lived with the symbols
The magic that leapt about his table
Lived not where he walked
But where he thought

In that sky to which Helena Blavatsky brought him
Demon Est Deus Inversus

.

In the dark you entered in 1939,
Did Plato and Plotinus welcome you?

Did your soul rise, a falcon in the air
Ignoring cries to bring it back to earth?

Did Cúchulainn honor you, show you the sword
That killed in battle frenzy the hound of Culain?

Did Emer soothe the wounds that ended you
And bind them deeply with a purple cloak?

Did honeybees ignore you in that dark
Where wild swans flew and fire sweetly burned?

Did all the gyres end, did darkness sing?
Did you become a consecrated bone?

.

Nothing is true, dear love, nothing is true.

.

and we look
to be understood,
do we not.
do we not wish
that something
of ourselves
should remain
even in the darkness
of what we call
"life"
even as we face
the death
that is always with us
the dark
shadow

that we cast
in brightest
sunlight
do we not
always wish it
to be loved, yes,
but to cast our consciousness
upon another
to live
in the words
another
breathes

for Deborah Bachals Schmidt

A MUTTER OF HOPKINS: A SONNET

Hippity Hop-
kins drowned in the verbal nerve of underovering
hovers in care of stepping stones to stop—
kin to the windhover, spring
flung down to plover.
I in heaven haven
mutter like a sound-struck lover
craven
before the final fierce
ecstasy of *ecce homo*—
Dolben's death pierce-
s the faith of Rome oh,
Seigneur, clutch
With Thy hands me, my sole soul, sweet touch

John Atkinson Grimshaw (1836-1893)
"Tree Shadows on the Park Wall, Roundhay, Leeds" (1870)

breathtaking
    I was thinking of you
the play of chiaroscuro
    when I saw this image
in this marvelous painting
    and of my own
of the path
    path
to nul'where
    throughout my
the dark, solitary
    long, long
figure,
    life,
the trees, the sky
    and the painting's
above
    beauty and deep
everything
    fragility

THE ARTFUL DARGER
after seeing *In the Realms of the Unreal* and the Darger exhibit at Seattle's Frye Museum

That's me—
    the little girl with the penis.
"There's a party upstairs?" "No, no, that's Henry—"
    the little girls forever in darger (danger!) (dagger!)
        some die violently
"Henry makes a lot of noise—"
    the little girls battle like men—epic—
"but only when he's alone. He'll never talk to you."

Fern disappeared after a while, walking down the road toward Zuckermans'. Her mother dusted the sitting room. As she worked she kept thinking about Fern. It didn't seem natural for a little girl to be so interested in animals. Finally Mrs. Arable made up her mind she would pay a call on old

Doctor Dorian and ask his advice. She got in the car and drove to his office in
the village.

Dr. Dorian had a thick beard. He was glad to see Mrs. Arable and gave her a
comfortable chair.

"It's about Fern," she explained. "Fern spends entirely too much time in the
Zuckermans' barn."

Henry can't draw
But he can trace.
He wishes to be a painter and must find a way
To put his magnificent visions on paper!
See the strangled little girl
Whose tongue is out as she dies,
Gasping.
What violence to Henry's "inner child"!

Henry paints pictures and makes stories—
      vast misspelled panoramas—
      no one sees or reads
(We are not individuals but choruses)
God is involved in these pictures and stories
Why does God never give Henry what Henry wants?
(Henry is Catholic and makes shrines to God;
            he entreats Him in a humble and heartfelt manner,
            though he also rails against Him;
Henry goes to Mass daily— sometimes several
            times daily—and takes the sacraments:
God stands in His Heaven and is Silent)

Henry pants after little girls
Henry and little girls are the same
      except for the burden of the penis
(There are no breasts in Henry's world)
      Except for the burden of the penis
                  he and the girls are the same, and they are both in *DANGER*
Henry can make girls that have no girl parts
but he is furious that God has imposed this terrible burden upon him
Henry is God
but he is also God's great enemy, the conscious artist.

Henry withdraws from the world.
He wishes to be a representational painter
but he is a representational painter who can't draw—
not a representational painter who draws badly
but a representational painter who can't draw at all.

He must transcend his limitations!
Henry, a janitor, is violently disturbed but keeps to himself so that no one except
God knows.
"I'm a hard-boiled egg," he says. He is also Humpty Dumpty—who fell.
He is crazy as a loon but he is not harmful except in the "realms" he inhabits—
"the realms of the unreal"—where he shoots and murders and rescues little girls
who have no sex,
whose legs are spread in utter panic as they run.

Saint Agnes, martyr, pray for me.

"Ben Weatherstaff," called out Mary, finding her breath. She stood below him
and called up to him with a sort of gasp. "Ben Weatherstaff, it was the robin who
showed me the way!"

Then it *did* seem as if Ben would scramble down on her side of the wall, he
was so outraged.

"Tha' young bad 'un!" he called down at her. "Layin' tha badness on a robin—
not but what he's impidint enow for anythin'. His showin' thee th' way inta the
garden! Him! Eh! tha' young nowt"—she could see his next words burst out
because he was overpowered by curiosity—"however i' this world did tha' get
in?"

"It was the robin who showed me the way," she protested. "It was the robin
who showed me the way."

At Jennie Richee. Hard pressed and harassed by the storm.
At Jennie Richee. Waiting for the blinding rain to stop.
At Cederine She witnesses a frightful slaughter of officers.

Here Henry is in his element—the air—
He rises to trace a flower—*l'absente de tous bouquets*
It is a task
performed in secret, sacred space night after night
He will never be anyone's father
He will only be these flowers
that grow in the empty nothing of consciousness
in a room no one will want to enter
in a loneliness that is nothing less than the entire visible world
(Henry wishes for a family, for his gone sister
    whose name he never found out)
His room is filled with children's books, books of adventure
God will save the children
Ug AK Gurg Gawk, I'm this thing getting choked

His world is the world of the Oz books turned round and darkened
He looks into the heart of the Emerald City
He is everyone and no one
Oh, God, grant me serenity, grant me grace of heavenly place, save me, salve,
for the waters come upon my soul, and I am lost too late too late
Lord, I have discovered no one wins the battle of life
and no one KNOWS—
What side was I on?
Darger (danger/darker) is everywhere

Oh, God (Deceiver)! Save me!

CODA

what is the difference
between a cowboy
and a soldier
what is the difference
in imagination
between a cowboy
and a soldier
what is the difference
for a boy
brought up
and trained
in the 1940s
trained
to be a boy
and a soldier
what is the difference
between a man
and a woman
for a boy
brought up
and trained
in the 1940s
(why do they argue so?)
what is the difference
between a boy
and a soldier
between a man

and a boy
between a man
and a woman
between a boy
who dreams
and a soldier
who wonders
will he escape
alive
will he escape
at all
who wishes he were a boy

who dreams
like the boy
of escape

and the cowboy
who rides
thru his dream

NOIR

after the enforced
regimentation
of the war
("You're in the Army now")
it must have seemed
possible
to return
to the notion
of the individual.
yet for many
it was not clear
what the overwhelming
situation
of "freedom"
would mean
for those
who had
practiced another trade
from 1939
to 1945.
The Maltese Falcon (1941)
was made during the war

and based on a novel
published in 1930.
The Big Combo (1955)
was made
ten years
after the war
had ended.
Shadow of a Doubt—
almost a defining
title for film noir—
was 1943.
Both *Laura*
and *Double Indemnity*
were 1944,
The *Lost Weekend*
1945.
Gilda,
with the great
George Macready,
was 1945.
Laird Cregar,
whose sexuality
was described
as "complicated"
and who was almost
a noir hero himself,
appeared in
Wake Up Screaming (1941),
This Gun for Hire (1942),
and *The Lodger* (1944)
before dying in 1944
in an ill-advised attempt
to slim down
to leading man
status.
to what extent
is homoeroticism
an element
of noir?
all of the villains
in *The Maltese Falcon*
are gay,
Sam Spade
the sole bastion
of heterosexuality

in the film.
is the noir hero's
masculinity
in a constant state
of questioning?
"Don't knock it
unless
you've tried it,"
a villain says
to Clint Eastwood
in *Dirty Harry* (1971).
"What makes you think
I haven't?"
answers Harry.
no one in the audience
thought he had.
In a Lonely Place
was 1950,
Ida Lupino's
The Hitch-Hiker
1953.
last night,
Sangye and I
watched
The Secret Garden (1949).
many of the film's
shadowy visuals
might qualify as noir
until, like the earlier
Wizard of Oz (1939),
it bursts into color
in the garden sequences.
if so, it would be the only noir film
to feature children—
immensely talented ones—
as its principal subject.
they are perhaps
among the few noir characters
who do not smoke.
and since chiaroscuro,
with all its ambiguity,
is of considerable importance
in noir,
at least one cinematographer
should be mentioned here.

Hungarian-born
John Alton,
one of the great
visual artists
of noir,
lived from
1901
to 1996.
his last film
was *Elmer Gantry* (1960):
contentious,
he left the industry
in 1962.
his book,
Painting with Light (1949),
remains a classic:
there are chapters on
"Mystery Lighting,"
"Special Illumination"
and "Visual Symphony."
singers Carly Simon
and Melissa Errico
have sought to create
noir through sounds,
through singing,
and of course songs,
usually performed
by women,
are often featured
in films noir:
Laura
is the face in the misty light.
Frank Sinatra,
another noir hero
who announced,
"I *am* Maggio,"
his character
in *From Here to Eternity* (1953),
co-wrote the song,
"I'm a Fool to Want You" (1951).
I was born in 1940:
noir was all around me
in my formative years.
I was fifteen when *Kiss Me, Deadly*
with the enigmatic box

containing the atom bomb
appeared.
Ralph Meeker
was the best of Mike Hammers.
did I give up noir
when I gave up cigarettes?
are we not all ultimately doomed?
isn't life a mixture of light and dark?
I don't know, baby,
but I can tell you this:
holding hands with my girlfriend, Sangye,
I still watch those films
in the darkness of my livingroom
(I live in noir)
in 2024.

TIM BURTON'S

Ed Wood
is about the
dream
not about the
product
the dream produces.
it's the kind of film
in which
someone has a dream,
follows it,
and produces
something wonderful:
Hitchcock,
John Ford,
Gershwin.
Ed Wood
has a dream,
follows it
and becomes—
"Worst Director
of All Time."
Burton's film
is about the dream
not about the product
the dream produces.

his dream
is the dream
of Hollywood,
the dream
of "the movies."
we all know that dream
of magic in the dark.
Wood is a man
for whom the dream
is everything,
who refuses to allow
reality
to have the upper hand.
he is physically
a man.
so what!
he can wear
women's
clothing
as he did
at his mother's
bidding
in childhood.
this man fought
in World War II,
did a man's
job,
but wore a pink
bra
and panties
under
his uniform.
childhood
and the child's
wonder
is everything.
the movies,
art
infantilize us
for certain moments,
allow the dream
to be realer
than what we know.
what we know
is that we will die.

the dream of art,
the dream of the movies,
the dream of all religions
tells us
that we will live.
that we will live.

FOR IVÁN AND JAKE
(FOR ADELLE AND NEELI)

who will write our epitaphs?
who will see the things
we failed to see
turn the corners
we were afraid to turn
who will know us
better
than we knew ourselves
though self knowledge
was our trade
who will see through
our self-deceptions
while maintaining
their own
will it be as it is for Yeats
whose fame is filtered through
a vast network of
what might be called
Professors of Misunderstanding
or as it is for Peyton Houston
who wrote brilliantly
but whose readers probably currently number
fewer than five
who will make the summarization
of our complicated and intertwined
lives
that we were too busy writing
ever to make
and which would have been filled
with fictions
in any case
(the muse inhabits
multiple worlds!)

who will read
our words
as *we* read them,
drawing their breaths
in pain
to tell
our story—
who will write
"the end"
to a book
that bears
our name?
and if there is
no end
no name?

NEELI, NEELI, NEELI
for Neeli Cherkovski (1945-2024)

an old friend
so strongly looking forward
to the imminent publication
of his work by City Lights—
suddenly stricken
by a heart attack.
one person says Thursday
one says Saturday.
"Jesse found him bleeding from the head
and thought it was only from that fall.
It wasn't until they got him to the hospital
that Jesse discovered he had
that heart attack."
"He's on life support
and it doesn't look good."
someone else says,
"induced coma."
what viciousness
the gods display
should they take
this moment of his
joy,

the moment in which
he understands his life's work
to be vindicated—
what contempt, what cruelty,
what carelessness of human toil
if they should take
this moment
from him.
live, Neeli, live.
.

3/19/24

goddam, Neeli, you didn't make it
goddam, Neeli, you didn't make it
goddam, Neeli, you didn't make it
not your fault, not your fault
nothing wrong with your heart
which was big and strong and open to all
not your fault, not your fault
you blamed yourself for so much
goddam, Neeli, you didn't make it
goddam, Neeli, you didn't make it
the heart in your body failed
not the heart in your mind
not the heart in the poetry
all of that lives
in everyone who knew you
in all who read you
goddam, Neeli, you didn't make it
goddam
goddam
may that book launch
be the biggest book launch
City Lights ever had
may all the poets, living and dead,
may Hank and Lawrence and Bob and Diane and Jack welcome you
and put their hands on your shoulders
and say what great work you did
may all your lovers all your lovers
(and who failed to love you?)
weep as I am weeping now
why did it take City Lights so long
to publish you?
no matter now.

all of the lights
of this great city
of san francisco
should be dimmed tonight
we have lost a luminary
we have lost
Neeli
still boyish in his 70s
still the poet
still the gay man
who wrote about so many
and whose words
gave heart
to all.
Whitman's wild child
goes home.

.

NEARLY...

upscale supermarket.
a woman is screaming,
"Neeli, hey, Neeli."
no sign of Neeli anywhere.
she screams again,
"Neeli, hey, Neeli."
I realize she is screaming at me.
"Excuse me, are you referring to
Neeli Cherkovski, the poet?"
I ask.
"Yes, yes. Hi, Neeli."
I explain that I am Jack Foley,
also a poet but not Neeli.
"I am not Neeli,"
I explain,
"only *Nearly*
Cherkovski."
The woman laughs.
"They hang together,"
she explains
to her boyfriend.

True story!

.

NEELI AGAIN

a younger poet friend,
in his late 70s,
surprised everyone
by dying.
the last time
I spoke to him,
he was certain
he was at
Death's Door
but the doctors
kept telling him
he was fine.
Neeli!—
turned out
you were
right.

AN INCANTATION FOR THE POET FRANCISCO X. ALARCÓN IN HIS SICKNESS (2016)

by "the divine" I mean
the longed-for
utterly impossible
ego-shattering
irreality

.

Francisco,
dear man,
named for the great saint Francesco
lover of Lady Poverty
you, lover of Lady Poetry
he, tamer of Brother Wolf
you, tamer of Brother Cancer

he, singer of the Canticle to the Sun
Altissimu, onnipotente bon Signore
you: *la luz da más luz*
I think of you
greeting the four directions
Tahui
"Which way is North?"
Which way is Love
Your breath stays with me:
poetry is the only cure
for the disease of life
poetry is the light
that is never lost
poetry is the soul's
chemotherapy.

my love to you, my friend
may poetry heal you
in tonatiuh in tlanextia *
light & love

            .

by "the divine" I mean
the longed-for
utterly impossible
ego-shattering
irreality

(whispered) VIVA LA VIDA

* Nahuatl: "May your sun shine forever"

RHETORIC

"We make out of the quarrel with others,
rhetoric,
but of the quarrel with ourselves,
poetry,"
famous lines by
William Butler Yeats.
for Yeats and other Modernists,

rhetoric
was the opposite
of poetry,
the linguistic practice
of politicians:
"oh, on my darling man."
yet, for the ancients,
rhetoric
was the art of discourse
logos, pathos, ethos.
it was a subject
of deep study,
the art of
persuasion.
what was "Howl"
when Allen Ginsberg
read it
in the Six Gallery
in 1955
but an exercise
in rhetoric?
what was the poetry
of Dylan Thomas?
in our time,
poetry is understood
as an adjunct
to music,
the "words" to a song,
but are there not moments
when at least some understand
that poetry
is music
and has no need
of "instruments"
other than the voice.
James Joyce
reading
from *Finnegans Wake,*
Robert Duncan
reading
from *Bending the Bow.*
Gertrude Stein:
"Would he like it
if I told him
If I told him

would he like it"—
at such moments
the joy of speech
which is the joy
of rhetoric
asserts itself.
Wikipedia: "Although some have limited rhetoric to the specific realm
of political discourse, many modern scholars liberate it to encompass
every aspect of culture. Contemporary studies of rhetoric address a
much more diverse range of domains than was the case in ancient
times. While classical rhetoric trained speakers to be effective
persuaders in public forums and institutions such as courtrooms and
assemblies, contemporary rhetoric investigates human discourse writ
large. Rhetoricians have studied the discourses of a wide variety of
domains."
it is here that poetry lives
in this "wide variety of domains,"
in the listening we grant
to the living,
to the always talking sea.

PAIRINGS

PAIRINGS is a sequence in which two (sometimes more) poems meet on the
page in the way that persons might meet on the street. For the most part, they
stand across the page from one another in the way that people stand across from
one another as they speak. They have things in common and things that separate
them. In many ways they illuminate each other. The "unit" in these pieces is not
the individual poem but the meeting—sometimes the collision—of the poems.

PAIRINGS: THE PATH OF THE OUTCAST

RICHARD FARIÑA   CORNELL

His sad life!   I entered the campus bookstore

I knew him a little at Cornell.
As the steward of "The Book and Bowl Club"
he poured wine into my glass.
We ran into each other occasionally on campus.
He gave an excellent performance in a wonderful
student production of *Under Milk Wood*.
He had a Harvard Book Bag,
which I thought was the coolest thing in the world.
He had published a story—in
The Evergreen Review, I believe.
It later came out in *New World Writing*.
Its title was "With a Copy of Dylan
Under My Arm."
The Dylan was Thomas,
Not Bob.
When he died,
I was still
Uncertain of everything.

intending to steal
some books.
I knew there were
plainclothes policemen
posted in the store.
they weren't hard to spot.
I saw one.
I was in—
what can I call it?—
a state,
had been for some time:
"conflicted."
I saw his eyes on me
as I went around the store
stuffing books
into my green
Harvard Book Bag.
I enjoyed
the excitement
I must have been causing
in the plainclothes
policeman.
I had a charge
account at the store.
I toyed with the possibility
of putting the books in my bag
on my charge account.
I chatted with the clerk
at the counter
turned
and walked towards
the door.
a strong hand
was on my shoulder.
I had chosen
the path
of the outcast.

PAIRINGS: BLAKE / GUESS WHO'S COMING TO

Two things from that long paper: the discovery
that "Blake" was an early spelling of
"Black": you can find it in both Skelton
and Chaucer: "nunnes blake," nuns

We watched *Guess Who's Coming to
Dinner*, a film I have always loved.
Everyone's wonderful, but Spencer
Tracy (the great white father!) is the

wearing black. So: "My mother bore me in the southern wild, / And I am BLAKE, but O! my soul is white." And this, on "Holy Thursday":

WE HAVE HERE—AS WE HAVE AT THE CONCLUSION OF "THE ECHOING GREEN"— A KIND OF GRADUAL FADING OF THE LIGHT IN WHICH THINGS ARE NO LONGER SEEN CLEARLY, AND IN WHICH THE SOUNDS WE "HEAR" TEND TO BECOME SOMEWHAT DISTANT: "ALL THE HILLS ECHOED." AT THIS POINT, I THINK, LANGUAGE BECOMES SOMETHING CLOSE TO PURE POTENTIALITY, TO PURE "SOUND" OR "MUSIC," TO THE "SONG" THAT THE PIPER PIPES. WHAT BLAKE IS ATTEMPTING TO MAKE US DO, I SUSPECT, IS TO TREAT *ALL* OF HIS WORDS IN THE SAME WAY THAT WE MUST TREAT THE NAMES OF HIS CHARACTERS: WE MUST CONTINUALLY RECOMBINE THEM, MUST TURN THEM AROUND AND AROUND IN OUR MINDS UNTIL THEY BECOME WORDS WHICH, THOUGH DIFFERENT, INVOLVING OTHER LETTERS, RETAIN IN THEIR SOUNDS THE ECHOES OF ONE ANOTHER. BLAKE HIMSELF USED WORDS OF THE BIBLE IN ORDER TO CREATE NEW HARMONIES, HARMONIES WHICH "CHIMED" WITH THOSE OF THE BIBLE, AND I THINK "HOLY THURSDAY" WAS MEANT TO SERVE THE SAME PURPOSE. TWAS ON A, FOR EXAMPLE, MIGHT EASILY BECOME TWAS HONOR, HOSANNA; THE SEATS OF HEAVEN, THE SAINTS OF HEAVEN, THE SEEDS OF HEAVEN; BENEATH THEM SIT, BE NEATH THEM SAID; WHITE AS SNOW, WHY 'TIS SNOW, WHY 'TIS NOW; TILL INTO, TELL UNTO, TOLL UNTO; THE VOICE OF SONG, THEY VOICE HIS SONG, THEIR VOICE IS SONG, THEIR VOICE, HIS SONG; THE FLOWERS OF LONDON TOWN, OR LAND ATONED, OR LENTEN TIME; BUT MULTITUDES OF LAMBS, BUT MULTITUDES OF LANDS, BUT MULTITUDES OF LIMBS, BOUGHT MULTITUDES OF LAMBS; THOUSANDS OF LITTLE BOYS, THOSE SANDS OF LITTLE BOYS; O WHAT A, O WATER; THE HUM OF MULTITUDES, THE HOME OF MULTITUDES, THE HYMN, THE HAM, THE HIM OF MULTITUDES; THEY LIKE THAMES WATERS FLOW, THEY LIGHT TIME'S WATERS FLOW, THEIR NIGHTTIMES WATERS FLOW; RADIANCE ALL THEIR OWN, RADIANCE ALL THEREROUND, RADIANCE ALL THEREON, REGENTS ARE THERE CROWNED; THE CHILDREN WALKING, THE CAULDRON WAKING, THE CALLED ARE WALKING; HARMONIOUS THUNDERINGS, OUR MOAN, HIS THUNDERINGS; THE VOICE, THE VOWS, THE JOY.

absolute center of the film. Tracy saying goodbye to Hepburn, to his career, to his audience, knowing he was near death even as he recited his lines.

When I first saw the film in 1967, I was in a *state*. I had been working madly, obsessively, intensely on a long paper on William Blake. I was more or less *crazed*, learning a lot, reading all sorts of things, unable to think of almost anything other than the paper, which was complex and stylistically adventuresome. I was, to put it another way, in a state of radical openness, though everything was fed back into the benign chaos of the paper. Given all that, the movie registered very powerfully. *It somehow told me that the work was worth it, no matter what.* (It was during this time that I had the insight about Yeats' "The Second Coming"—that the opening lines were not an image of chaos but an image of escape.)

Was it Tracy's famous speech? The daring of the film? I don't know. I delighted in the movie. And delighted in the gift it gave me. "All the hills echoed."

PAIRINGS: THE ROCK

THE ROCK

I have friends who have returned
to the religion of their youth
no doubt from a different point of view
but they have returned nonetheless.
at 83 I wish I could join them
but I don't seem able to do it,
especially with the considerable
number of erring Fathers
and even erring Sisters
appearing in the Catholic Church,
people who perhaps had hoped that
enforced chastity would subdue
the desperate urgings they felt
and who then discovered
that the Church provided them
with new opportunities for passion's expression.
I was asked once if I had considered
becoming a priest.
a poet is as close as I could come.
we are put on earth
first to keep ourselves alive
and then perhaps
to make discoveries,
to learn about the place in which
unknowing ("thrown") we find ourselves
abandoned. we make such discoveries
or fail to make them
in the time we have
and then we're bundled off
into whatever it was we were
—if it was anything—
before our birth.
the task is thought
and making.
we are creatures of possibility
and the making
of the possible
into the real.
I understand my friends'
delight in story
and the wish to turn
story into fact.
if I could join them
if I could join them
I surely would,
but I am a lone rock

FATHER O'FONDLE

comes to town
Hoping that your pants are down
What's your sport, me lad, says he
Can you sit upon me knee
(I have sport enow for thee!)
Let me look upon your dangle
Try Confession from THIS angle
What I beat is not a drum
Who put the "cum" in "Vobiscum"?
(Which of you dare call me "scum"?)
Bishop, Bishop, though I'm lacking
I know you will send me packing
To another parish bright
Where I'm sure I'll do all right
I'll bring "God" to them and theirs
And they'll remember in their prayers
In the night when dreams are wet
They will see me smiling yet
Holding out God's helping hand—
There's a sweet and sacred band!
Till Hell turns to ice and freezes
You'll make Love to me—and Jesus
I'll apply the priestly arts
To your troubled private parts
Here, my lad, 's a welcome solace
Let me touch your throbbing phallus
Hear the Sacred Choir thrumming
As I prepare my Second Coming!
Father O'Fondle, troubled man
Needing love, and under ban
In such desire for the Son,
Would I have done
        as you have done?

...

tonight I saw a film
(*Spotlight*)
about those who pollute
the great experiment in thought
that constitutes
Catholicism.
I do not speak
as a believer.

by the seaside
not unhappy with my
state
waiting for the waters
to grind me down.
whatever
brought us here
is not omniscient
but has a great need
to
discover
itself,
to know
its ins
& outs,
its circuits
& limitations.
"I could make you," the voice said
in the dream,
but I could not prevent you
from dying.

I am not
a believer.
but the pollution
the filth
is wide and deep.
it is heartbreaking.
it is heartbreaking.
"Have you become a
Protestant?"
"Why would I renounce
an absurdity that is
logical & coherent
for an absurdity that is
illogical & incoherent?"
Augustine. Aquinas.
Theresa. Dante.
Francis ("Fioretti").
J.F. Powers.
J.R.R. Tolkien.
Father Yarwood in
Port Chester.
The innocent
Believer.
—all, all tainted

PAIRINGS: SIBLINGS

FOR VETERANS DAY 2023: MY UNCLE WAYNE

Or "Herbert"
Never heard my father
Refer to him as "Herbert,"
The name on his
Discharge papers.
Perhaps that was
Another brother…?
But my father was
"John" and "Jack"
And on a postcard to his mother
"Harold."
Names slip easily
From one to another.
Wayne
Died after his discharge
From a foul, murderous war,
Discharged

FOR ANDREAS WEILAND

Micha ist Mittwoch Abend gestorben
words from another language that I
barely understand
but I know what they mean.
Micha, my friend's brother,
died Wednesday evening.
it is Thursday evening now
so the world has been without Micha
for a day.
the birds and animals he fed will wonder,
his kindness suddenly ended.
can we tell them,
as his brother told me,
Micha ist Mittwoch Abend gestorben.
two dear men, living on the edge
of poverty
in a deep forest

A hundred plus years ago: 1919
Dead ninety plus years ago: 1929?
38 years old?
The photo of my father
In my hallway: 1926.
Was Wayne alive then?
The discharge says nothing
But the family knew:
Mustard gas
Murdered Wayne.
Older, he had brought my father
And their sister
Into show business
And though my father loved him
He could not bring himself
To see his brother as he lay dying
And calling for my father.
My father named me for him in 1940
And, later, followed him
Into a military cemetery
(1967).
No photos.
They're all gone
My father's family—
Francis, May, Goldie, Wayne ("Herbert"?),
John Harold Aloysius ("Jack")—
What is left but the name,
"Descendants of the Marauder."
"Foley Square"
Where I got married
Over sixty years ago
Named for still another Foley, "Big Tom"—
Another Foley I never met!
They are leaves
Fluttering in the spaces
Of my mind
Slipping away
Into the wind.
And now Adelle among them.
A friend recently quoted Randall Jarrell:
"We suffer pain and call it wisdom
But it is not wisdom:
It is pain."

but with entwined imaginations
and abiding love.
it was Wednesday, a cruel Wednesday
in November,
2023.
I do not believe in souls
but I do believe
that everything
is affected by everything else
and that Micha's kindness
was a flame
in the German night.

THE BROADWAY THOROUGHFARE
for Aunt Goldie

Goldie, Goldie
            you're a girl you're a girl
Back in the teens
            you're a beautiful girl
Of the century now
            head's a-whirl head's a whirl
Kaput—
            for this beautiful pearl

You are somewhere
            you're a peach you're a peach
In this photo
            you cld pose at the beach
But I don't know
            in the swim in the swim
Where
            you cld get in the swim

Briefly met

When I was a child
        can we kiss can we kiss
And you an old woman
        can I steal only one?
You had your moment
        'twould be bliss 'twould be bliss
Of glamor
        will you be my sweet hon'
Never a star
        see the stars see the stars
But a dependable chorus girl
        shining right on our love
And a Ziegfeld dancer—
        we'll be stars we'll be stars
"A swell-lookin' dame."
        and we'll shine up above—
Do a turn
        COME ON, ma honey bun
For me,
        come on, ma sweet
Goldie—
        you don't need money, hon'
Now!
        tappin' your feet
Shine gold gold gold
        wearin' tights
Like an old-time
        in the nights
Penny
        on the BROADWAY THOROUGHFARE

PAIRINGS: FOR JUNO GEMES
& ROBERT ADAMSON
12/15/22

dove sta memoria
that place in the mind
where love stays
there we remember
what is etched forever
as long as mind lasts
written in book
or solitary
poem
spoken to the air
to loved one.
death cannot grasp it
so long as mind lasts.
we live to remember, live
to write things down
in this fabulous
"book"
that changes
like the changing
moon

when two
who were one
become only
one
when the great separator
severs the knot
and they are no longer
bound to one
another
when death parts
one from other,
then deep night
enters
and reassuring
fictions
vanish,
then we know
time
as it is:
the open
wound
that nothing
can fill

PAIRINGS 96: JOLSON / STEINWEG

ABOUT A QUARTER TO NINE

**WHEN MARCUS STEINWEG
QUOTES FOUCAULT...**

have you thought
what it means
to remember
a song,
to find a song
"catchy"?

how
can anyone say
he stands
anywhere
but
at the edge

take the great 1935
Al Dubin-Harry Warren
song,
"About a Quarter to Nine"
sung brilliantly
(and, thankfully, mostly not in blackface)
by Al Jolson.
what we wish to remember
is an arresting *phrase*:
"The stars
are gonna come out and shine
tonight
about a quarter to nine."
the phrase, both words and music
but especially the music,
expresses wonder, delight,
even amazement
but the event it refers to
hasn't happened quite *yet*.
the phrase
both is the event
and is the prelude
to the event.
we will hear the phrase again
in the next eight bars,
which begin,
"My loving arms...."
the composer
forces us to wait
three strongly emphasized syllables
before he allows us to hear
the equivalent of "stars"—
the word "arms."
what we call a "song"
is a ritualized structure
that creates both desire
and a means by which desire
may be problematically
satisfied.
the next eight bars—
the "release"—
remove us from the phrase entirely
but with a promise to return.
"what" we desire
is a phrase of music
but desire is desire
and may be easily
redirected.
"A pretty girl,"
wrote Irving Berlin,

of the abyss,
in the warm
kiss
of the night
wind
that will
tear him apart.
we do not
expect
wisdom
from Steinweg
who knows
that
wisdom
is nothing but
the status quo
wearing green
as if
it were Irish.
he recognizes
le néant
towards which
thought rushes,
as to the arms
of a loving
mother

who will smile
and sing to him
and kiss the wounds
that turn him to dust.
thr gsbot bivyim yhr derryinhd yhr nounfsty

[The concluding line of the above poem is
from a poem of mine that is dedicated
to the sixth Marx Brother: Typo.]

...

ADORABLE WITH FOUCAULT

Only the thought that "does not bind itself in
advance to the sworn rules of the game of
science," has a chance to be scientific at all. This
is where philosophy operates. She is neither
science nor beyond her. She stops at the edges
of the knowledge devices to demonstrate
their fragility. There are sentences that with
denial of knowledge lead to expansion of
knowledge. You can find them in all texts of the

"is like a melody."
the desire for the phrase
and the desire for the woman
merge
in a longing
that is simultaneously
deeply satisfied
and deeply frustrated.
music
brings us
into the world again,
awakens us
to the constant longing
that accompanies
our being.
not now but
"Tonight
about a quarter
to nine."

...

history of Philosophy. They are painful or
amusing. Often they border on nonsense. They
always have an energy value that makes them
seem questionable. University philosophy
ignores them as best it can, which can hardly
succeed, because their factuality is indisputable.
So you argue with a lack of seriousness. The
sentences did not express a serious statement,
etc. This is how you put philosophical
conservatism on display...There are thousands
of such sentences. One of them is from Foucault,
who reconciles reason with madness: "Every
light dies by the day it brought about, and is so
given back to the night that tore it apart."
—Marcus Steinweg

SWANEE (the song)
Or, What George Gershwin,
Irving Caesar and
Al Jolson Did...
    a review

did you know
that the original opening line
of Stephen Foster's
"Ethiopian Melody,"
"Old Folks at Home"
(since 1935 the state song
of Florida),
was "Way down upon
the Swanee Ribber,"
thus combining
a deliberate mispronunciation
of both the river's name, Suwannee,
and the word, "river."
revisions to the lyric

occurred later (2008)
but the melody
remained
a sentimental, nostalgic ballad.
still, a question
might arise:
how would one
get back to
"the old folks at home"?
one could hardly walk:
one would take the train.
George Gershwin knew
that the rhythm of the train
(which later inspired
not only his great
"Rhapsody in Blue"
but hundreds of thousands of songs
about "choo choos")
was not the rhythm
of a sentimental ballad
but the fierce, all-powerful
rhythm of the new god
of the twentieth century:
speed.
"I've been away from you a long time"
BOOM BOOM BOOM
"I never thought I'd miss you so,
Somehow I feel
Your love is real—
Near you I wanna be.
The birds are singing, it is song time"—
the masterful verse
explodes into a chorus
that is power personified,
a perfect song for Al Jolson
whose blackface make-up
told us that he was something like
the enfeebled "Old Black Joe"
but whose nervous, violent
energy
thrust at the audience,
engaging it at every moment,
denied everything that the make-up told us
was true.
it was a moment of birth

in which power
in the form of "the black man"
came forward to tell us
(tell us from the mouth of the outcast,
the despised one, the trod upon,
the enslaved—
not only the African
but the Jew)
that in our heart of hearts
we were not "dark"
but fabulous
rainbows,
that the voice of one of us
(one from the "lower" east side,
the dregs of New York City)
could rise up
in all its power
and be the voice
of all.
what Jolson was about
was the transformation
of darkness into power.
in the darkness
of the theater
his I flowed into us
and made us
no longer slaves
but men.
"...in D- I- X- I- E ven
though my Mammy's
waitin' for me..."
"The folks up North
will see me no more
when I get to the
Swanee shore."
Waken, waken. *

---

* Note: my attempt to describe Al Jolson's effect on his audience should not
be taken as an approval of his wearing blackface. As is often said, blackface is
bad now and it was bad then. Nonetheless, unfortunately, it is part of our
performance history.

PAIRINGS: LORCA

FOR A FRIEND

thinking of you
in Andalusia
and of Lorca
a sad wind
"the street life
is social and vivid"
-trying to remember
his childhood prayers
"the orange trees
are green"
"moorish arches
and reflecting pools"
-as he walked
towards the horrendous death
reserved for him
"roman walls"
Sevilla
green
a sad wind
a sad wind
a sad wind
a sad wind among the olive trees

"old man
with your beard
full of butterflies
beautiful as the mist
voice a column
of ash
boys stripped to the waist
by the East River
the Bronx
corduroy shoulders
frayed by the moon
New York of wire and death
a bird
its sex pierced by a needle
your beard luminous
and chaste
maricas
men of the green glance
sleep sleep sleep
dream of being a river
sleeping like a river
lover of the body
nothing remains
America
drowns in machines
& lament—
   the kingdom of wheat
   is here"

PAIRINGS: BORGES

THE MAN WHO WAS BORGES

AFTER BORGES'S "THE ART OF POETRY"

Oedipus Rex
was the first detective story.

*Looking at a woman's face
We see the color of dreams,*

as in many detective stories,
the detective
and the criminal
merge
and a woman
plays a significant role.
when the supernatural enters,
as in Poe's "Murders in the Rue Morgue"
or Conan Doyle's "The Hound of the
Baskervilles,"
the author usually
naturalizes the supernatural
and offers an explanation
that covers all the bases.
but what if the explanation
is inadequate? what if it fails
to explain
everything?
mightn't that lead us
(as in G.K. Chesterton's novel,
The Man Who Was Thursday)
into a deeper
mystery?
I found
the same thing to be true
when I read Borges'
great story,
"Death and the Compass,"
in which the
"natural"
explanation
is questionable.
what more can be said?
at the heart
of the words
is something
to which
the words
can only
point.

   .

The face of a woman we see only in dreams
Which is our own face,

Gazing back at us as in a mirror,
And the sound of a voice echoing
In our consciousness, echoing
From the face in the mirror,

Or as we lay dreaming in deep sleep
And only our fantasy moves us to action,
We discover the possibilities of action
In the vast overriding river we call sleep

That protects us from the world
As a poem does, as the world is, in a poem,
Vast, echoing, inhabiting the poem,
A sweet, green, ululating world.

Borges's beautiful, elegant lines
Bring us into the pastiche of his thought
And into the images haunting his thought
As a river moves in wayward, wandering lines,

And my love, like a river, is a wonder
Drawing me deeply to a woman named Sangye,
And to my knowledge that the word "Buddha"
                 is the meaning of "Sangye."
And to the vast River that Time is, and

               to wonder

AFTERGLOW

Siempre es conmovedor el ocaso
por indigente o charro que sea,
pero más conmovedor todavía

es aquel brillo desesperado y final
que herrumbra la llanura
cuando el sol último se ha hundido.
Nos duele sostener esa luz tirante y distinta,
esa alucinación que impone al espacio
el unánime miedo de la sombra
y que cesa de golpe
cuando notamos su falsía,
como cesan los sueños
cuando sabemos que soñamos.

AFTERGLOW

Sunset always moves us,
whether it is gaudy or impoverished,
but even more moving
is that last luminosity, desperate and final,
that turns the plain to the color of rust
when the sun has finally
                    gone down.
We have trouble enduring that tense, distinct light,
that hallucination which imposes on space
the unanimous human fear of shadows—
and which stops suddenly
when we see its falseness,
as dreams end
when we see we are dreaming.

—Spanish by Borges; translation by me.

PAIRINGS: POET, TREE

fig tree	ogden nash
winding round	wrote lyrics
thyself, fabulous	to a Broadway
presence,	flop: *Nash at Nine.*
reaching into world	there may have been

unencumbered,
deep-rooted monument
to what is here for ages and ages,
user of time,
breather
of the same air
as I—
rootless,
transitory,
envying thy wonderful
and passionate
embeddedness.

*

it was in my time
that American leaders
could not agree
about fundamental
principles.

an original cast
recording
but it has gone the way
of the dodo &
the dinosaur.
one thing only
emerges from it:
a word:
it was not a "musical"
it was, wrote Nash, a *wordsical.*
in all our passionate
devotedness
to sound
& meaning,
to music
& thought,
do we not,
poets,
write words
& wordsicals
that vanish
into air?

PAIRINGS: PANDEMONIUM

PANDEMONIUM

someone asks
what to call
the horrific era
in which we live.
I think the answer
is abundantly
clear:
PANDEMONIUM
all the demons
have been let loose
to cry
their *ignis fatuus*
cries

what can the artist do
but seek
for what Wallace Stevens called
"ghostlier
    demarcations,
keener
    sounds"

PAIRINGS: NOW (03/04/2024)

ANECDOTE

the great elephant
    there was a fire
of growing old.
    in my kitchen today.
I will say it again:
    I didn't know about it
the great
    until Sangye woke me
elephant of
    to tell me of it.
growing old.
    she had managed
the elephant
    with some help
of growing.
    from workmen-friends
the great
    who had been doing
elephantine
    yard work outside
experience
    to put
of
    the fire out
growing old.
    and dispose of
this is
    the ashen remains
the elephant.
    of a useless, forgotten pile of papers
this is
    that had been
growing.
    next to the stove,
this is growing
    the place where
old.

MORNING SONG OF IMPOTENT POTUS (2018: REMEMBER)

King Liar sits in a house
    of White
King Liar visits the land
    with Blight
Unevenly does this man
    dispense
And by his side is the
    foul fool Pence

Chaos, says Liar, is what
    I am
A man of business,
    my business Sham
I say I'm an ordinary guy
    like you
But even the dogs know
    it isn't true.

My orange hair feels
    the lack of Hope
Sometimes I flatter, sometimes
    I grope
I have a wife and a son
    in law
Who drinks Russian vodka
    and flouts the law

The law, c'est moi, says
    busy Liar
Watch me burn with
    my pants on fire,
I know for what you fools
    are yearning
But look, the country is
    burning. Burning!

the fire
we are
    that finally
elephantine (Elephantidae!)
    posed no danger
too.
    began.

PAIRINGS: POETS / DECEMBER BIRTH LIGHT

FOR LUCILLE LANG DAY, 12/5

It's all about light, your birthday,
all about the possibility of illumination.
Your name carries with it
a slightly diabolical overtone:
Lucifer (light bearer) / Lucy.
I've always thought
it had to do with your willingness
to take risks.
Fearless, you challenge whatever
is dead or deadening in the world:
you can be deeply loving
but fierce in rage as well.
That is the true meaning
of your name, the one which
defines you
not only as a woman
but as a force: Lucy, Lucifer,
bringer of light.

DECEMBER 10
for Joe Masi

Hey, Joe,
It's your birthday
And HER birthday too—
The strangest
And most evasive
Of American poets,
Emily Dickinson.
And in today's mail
Came *In the Realms
Of the Unreal,*
A documentary about
That strangest
Of American
Artists, the amazing
Henry Darger,
Laureate
Of little girls.
Emily and Henry,
Two great reclusive
Failures
Whom crushing Time
Redeemed—
Famous only after
The shadows
Took them
In their arms.

Proof that light
Can shine on us
At any time
And that what matters
Is the work
And what Pound called,
Aptly and truly,
"The quality
Of the
Affection."

P.S.
And you—you are from Port Chester
Don't let them ride Port Chester
It's famous for you

(I know you know the tune)

...

FOR AMOS WHITE 12/10

Hey, Amos. It's that day again—a day you share with another poet of
renown, Ms. Emily Dickinson, though I doubt that the lady in white could
have done the duets that you, Mr. White, can do sooooooooo well. No jazz
back in those days. Do you know the old Fats Waller joke about the
drunken cockroach? "Beat me, Daddy, I just *ate* the bar." No bars for you
but a great big tongue-tickling cake. Hope it's been a grand day.

...

AT WATER'S EDGE 12/11
For Dave Mason

"How are we to live if we only read
ourselves? We have to look beyond one life

to the many lives of all the dead and living.
I think of you, your mastery of voice

I love and live in opposition to.
I think of the constant noise our species makes."

dear man,
who roamed the world
from Bellingham, WA
to Tasmania.
what circularities!
I read your poetry
for the life
it always manifests.
I know of no one
who loves the world
as you do,
who recognizes
the living element
in everything
he sees.
"scuddings of shadow
and the last starlight dropped
in the gum tree grove."
what syllables
you make!
grandfather now,
you watch that lovely being
with an adoration
that does not deny
delight.
I think at last I know
what moves me
so deeply
in your work:
I saw it clearly
in the film, *Pacific Light*:
the always actualizing presence
of love,
love for the earth
and love for every creature
that lives its life
at water's edge.

...

TODAY IS THE BIRTHDAY OF THE POET,
JEROME ROTHENBERG:
L'CHAIM!
12/11

Jerry, Jerry, Jerry
Our red mountain
Knew from the beginning
It was not necessary
To believe the received
Wisdom.
It was necessary
To find models
That could stimulate
The heart's need
For articulation.
Where could one find
The breathing in
That leads to speech
And honor.
Look to the unremembered
Look to the improperly
Translated
Discover the avant-garde
In the deep past
In the mouths
Of the long dead
& unregarded.
Find *poetics*
In the dust
We barely realized
Cried out
Beneath our feet.

NONAGENARIAN!

May there be no need of bars:
Just night, revolution, stars.

HAPPY BIRTHDAY & LOVE
from Jack & Sangye

...

[What is the status of the poet?
What can be said of the poet's impact
If any?
For most of America and perhaps
The world
Song lyrics are their only poetry.
How can we regain
The lost dignity
Of the poem?
Tous les poètes
Sont Orphée:
Son histoire
Est l'histoire de tous.]

REQUIEM 2024

how does one name the holy

argument as to the "emotional content" of poetry
perhaps the terminology is wrong
perhaps all terminology is wrong

we are
friends
but we argue
about
poetry
among
other
things

god who are you anyway

terminations
blind alleys?
he told me about L=A=N=G=U=A=G=E poetry

what good is an argument if nothing comes of it
is self-expressiveness enough
does it matter that I write at the computer
what is the Final End   of anything?
trick me into believing
all fuckin right baby
why did he call her baby

we are
friends
but
we
argue

who is that person
the violence of his language suddenly transforming him into someone I never knew

and that other
who wishes to "use" me

who are they
who tell me
things

who speak in a language which is constantly in flux
they tell me
about "voice" in poetry

they tell me
about "writing" and its advantages over "voice"

they tell me
nothing new
but they talk
constantly
and their
voices
will not
be

still

how does one name the holy
is it through silence
does the holy exist at all until it is named

so many
dead persons
so much
stillness

I saw you at the theater
I saw you at the coffee house later

poor evelyn nesbit
"stanford white was the only man I ever loved"

my friend larry "in the first hours of his sainthood"
jan kerouac (the tragedy of that family)
all the dead ones
do they continue
to argue
does it matter what they believed
alive

do they, dying, break through to the holy
did my father break through to the holy
did my mother
or my uncle panny
or my aunt maggie who called my dead mother "beloveded sister"
I can't remember them doing anything but arguing

can you tell the difference between my family and a loony bin?
you have to apply to get into a loony bin

and that woman in the loony bin whom I have never forgiven
for failing to encourage my poetry
have I been to see her in her agony
have I phoned her at least
is *she* in the realm of the holy

requiem
rest in peace
requiescat in pace
go to heaven

the soldier
caught in the mist;
the boy

helping him;
the huge
statue
of the buddha

here,
love does not enter the question

the argument
with my friend

the man does not speak at all
until the moment when he is
bayoneted to death:
"Oh no...please...please..."

This film director
made a "Western" which,
it was said,
"looked like it took place in Southeast Asia"

this requiem
is for all the dead, all
but it is necessarily
speech of the living

so many dead

and there was difficulty *understanding*

beloved, beloved, beloved

He asked me, Can you do it?
Can you spend all that time on the phone?
There's plenty of money in it for you
"I didn't care
I had a family to support,"
he said

so his writing
didn't matter

"Go to her," she wrote me, "you will never have another chance,
you will regret it later if you do *not* go"
And so I went
not because of the letter
but because of my entire mangled childhood

my mother showed me the scar from her radiation treatment
"It was terrible," she said, flashing her eyes at me, a theatrical
but effective gesture
Typical
of childhood abuse
survivors
to develop
multiple
personalities:
good mother, bad mother
this one
loves me
and there is a child who relates to this one
this one
hates me
and there is a child who relates to this one too
twin
sisters
how can we tell them apart? (*requiem*)
either one may appear (*requiem, a solemn mass for the*
spirits of the dead, may they rest in peace)
either mother may offer herself for an embrace

who are you, mother?
and, if you know, who am I?

Wit
masking
coldness
Intelligence
masking
indifference
Yet I was in tears

[—Upset because the baby was crying
(and she didn't know why)
she said to the baby, me,
"Now you'll have something to cry *about*"
As she hit me, hard]

what is the "emotional content" of poetry?
what do we "feel" as we "read" a poem?

Comme un voleur de nuit, chez vous, la mort avide
S'est glissée... Is it death in the silences?
Is it death in the whiteness
as we congratulate ourselves

at piecing together these black marks—
black, here, being equivalent to "life"—
is it mind we feel
in its radical freedom
in its sudden power
"comme un voleur de nuit"

De l'enfant rose et blond il va se faire un ange
Of the child rosy and blonde he makes an angel

We are angels of reading

We read
the book of the blue sky
which masks
the blackness
and infinity
of "space"

Our home is with the infinite—no?

—And then she warned me about women:
Watching a film:
"You see what a woman can do"
When I objected, "But, Mom, you're a woman"
she answered, "That's different."

"As from omen we get ominous, so from numen we derive numinous.
I shall speak, then, of a unique 'numinous' state of mind, which
is always found wherever the category is applied.
This mental state is irreducible to any other, and therefore,
like every absolutely primary and elementary datum,
while it admits of being discussed, it cannot be strictly defined.
There is only one way to help another to an understanding of it.
He must be guided and led on by consideration and discussion
of the matter through the ways of his own mind, until he reaches
the point at which 'the numinous' in him perforce begins to
stir, to start into life and into consciousness.
Our X cannot, strictly speaking, be taught, it can only be
evoked."

How do we *call* spirit?
how do we "catch"
breath?
You listen, she said, and it's gone
faster even than
life

(which also
goes)
"breaths' burial"
wrote Gustaf Sobin
about
his
book of poetry

a friend, a poet, at eighty
had open heart
surgery
"Do whatever you need
to make me
well"
The last time we spoke
he quoted Chaucer to me
the count
of syllables
like the beat
of
his
heart
as he lay
on the table
fearing
the "double bind"
of death
(damned if you do
damned if you don't)
He said to me once, "I live
between a bar
and a mortuary."

The need
for the
numinous
to arise
in *one's own*
consciousness

and you,
love,
the one who breathes beside me
nightly
may you not fear
(is love fear?)

"He dwells, says St. Paul, in an unapproachable light.
Observe here the exactitude of St. Paul's expression...
For he says not merely in an incomprehensible, but
(what conveys far more) in an altogether 'unapproachable'
light...A sea into which divers may plunge, but which they
cannot fathom, would represent the merely 'incomprehensible.'
It would only represent the 'unapproachable' if it remained in
principle beyond search and beyond discovery. *And this line
of thought draws him imperceptibly farther.* The bounds
of the 'incomprehensible' are extended, and the whole
numinous consciousness is set astir in it, one element
in the feeling prompting to the others.

"We call it 'incomprehensiblility' and distinguish from it
the 'inapprehensibility' which springs not from the 'exceeding
greatness' but from the 'wholly otherness' of God, from what
is alien and remote in Him, from what we have
called the '*mysterium stupendum.*'"

Words
enter the body of language
with no guarantees
and no
closure

The poet's words
enter the
openness
of that
enormous
interpretative
activity
which
we
call
"literature"

We read
the book of the blue sky
which masks
the blackness
and infinity
of "space"

I held her down and she screamed,
"Give it to me, oh, fuck, give it to me, now, now, ah, sweet, sweet—"
Her sweet sighs told me she had not only come

but
bled. O!
She lay there naked
suffering
and totally
satisfied
Touch me here.
O what pain.
Touch me here.
O.
Burn me.

a "savior"
bleeding
like a woman at her "period"
dying
in an orgy
of
suffering
"It is Love on the cross," she said,
"Love dying in agony
penetrated
screaming
like a w-
oman
at a departing
sailor: 'Why have you
for-
saken
me?'"

we are
light
coming to consciousness
of
itself
bright light
men & women
of light

what is mind
but light?
what is body?

Walking,
I vanish into light—

Kora—the seed—
above ground—under—
                          the need
to follow her—down the rabbit hole
                              following the
idea
of resurrection—
                  seed-
time vanishes/returns   we grow
in branch and root
in winged or finny stuff
or cloven hoof
in bird-
sound, animal alarm or
pleasure
describe a scene—
scene vanishes—
mind appears—
Kora   woman
under
ground
                        No need
that is not satisfied
of food
or sex—

The American actor Tyrone Power
so handsome in *Captain from Castile*
at 44 began to look
remarkably like Richard Nixon

voices
saying,
"You've written this
before, this is old
stuff, these techniques
are ancient history,
what do you know
that's
new?"
Yet these
worn-out
techniques
are
all
I
have:

something
to
begin
with,
the
basis
of
whatever
"new"
I come to

In Tennessee Williams'
Baby Doll
Caroll
Baker
sucking
her
thumb:
the
infinitely
desirable
child-bride
"I'll be twenty tomorra"
"Lie down,"
she tells Eli Wallach,
playing a stereotypical Sicilian
("We are an ancient people," he says,
"Mama mia," he says—this
from a "master of language"!)
"Lie down,"
she says, "in mah crib."

.

requiem

.

requiem

Do I speak harshly to you, love
am I indifferent
or cold

not because of something
you have done
but because
of something you have done
in my dreams

"When you know *everything* you are like a dark sky.
Sometimes a flashing will come through the dark sky.
After it passes, you forget all about it,
and there is nothing left but the dark sky."

The end
Of the Twentieth Century:
I awoke this morning
burdened by history

How does one name
the holy
in this radical
freedom
in this moment
scarcely moment
this *flash*
of
freedom,

everything
goes

and we are everywhere
open
alive
speaking
to one another
in loving
converse

requiem

requiem

what emerges now?
what politics?
what gender questioning?
I am not a "white male"
I am a European American
of *deliberately unspecified gender.*

DEAR MR. GUTMAN,

I understand
that you are interested
in acquiring
a famous
statuette
of a black
bird,
a "dingus,"
as Mr. Spade
called it.
I am writing to tell you
it is available
on the internet
for a very
reasonable price.
You will be happy to know
you will not have to murder anyone
or betray them to the police
in order to acquire it.
I have one
and am very pleased
with it.
Noticing it
in my parlor,
a friend wondered
what I was doing
with a raven
in my living room.
I explained that the source
was not Edgar Allen Poe
but Dashiell Hammett.
I told him that birds
were a sign
of good luck.
I realize that your resources
may be extremely limited
at this time
but perhaps you might persuade

one of your associates
(I understand
that you have made it all up with
Wilmer)
to give it to you
as a birthday present.
Yours in Ornithology,
Jack.
P.S. I am sending a copy
of this letter
to Mr. Joel Cairo
and to Ms.
Bridget O'Shaughnessy.

FINIS

LIFE WITH LUIGI

when Rosie Fistula
do the hoolah baloolah
it's not-a the same
as-a the nuns in-a the school-a
(bet you' pastafazoola!)
I give-a da posy
to beautiful Rosie
she's a sweet-a coquette
when she eat da spaghett'

...

where do people go
when they die?
they go to the movies.
how can you doubt it?
last night I saw
Sunset Boulevard:
Gloria Swanson,
William Holden,
Erich Von Stroheim,
all dead.
the director dead too.
I saw Gregory Peck,
Gregory Ratoff,
Jean Arthur,
Irene Dunne,
James Stewart,
Eddie "Rochester" Anderson,
S.Z. "Cuddles" Zackall,
Elisha Cook, Jr.,
Betty Hutton,
Judy Garland,
Emlyn Williams,
William Demarest,
Paul Robeson,
Keye Luke,

Henry Hull,
Mischa Auer,
James Barton,
Bobby Driscoll,
Margaret Hamilton,
Ethel Barrymore,
John Barrymore,
Ethel Waters,
Henry Fonda,
Gene Kelly,
Cyd Charisse—
all there in the movies,
all dead.
where do people go
when they die?
they go to the movies.

...

CAPO DI TUTTI I CAPOS

Are you not capo di tutti i capos?
Nah, nobody's capo di tutti i capos.
Who are you then? I thought you were capo di tutti i capos.
I'm a respectable businessman.
A businessman?
Yeah, a businessman.
What business are you in?
I'm in the export business.
Oh? What do you export?
Men.
Two armed men enter. The sound of shots.
A body slumps to the floor.
Men. I export men. To hell. You'll find the capo di tutti i capos there.
Sound of the tape recorder being turned off.

...

MAESTRO

is someone conducting
bernstein
as he turns
in his grave

...

THE ONE THE ONLY

I saw Groucho Marx's live show in San Francisco
sometime in the early 70s.
an audience member
asked him about someone who
evidently worked for him.
"Hey, Groucho, how about...[the name of the person]?"
Groucho repeated the name and added,
without missing a beat,
"She doesn't count. She's a Schvartze."
the audience simply laughed—
no one objected—
but the remark
didn't make it to the record.
are Schvartzes authority figures?
there was a reason why
You Bet Your Life
was taped.
Groucho was a loose cannon
and might say
anything:
taping the show
allowed the producers
to eliminate
remarks like that.
"I can't believe
I know Groucho Marx!"
said star-struck Dick Cavett.
especially in the later days,
the character Groucho played
could be sentimentalized

and often was.
people justified his attacks
as "deflating authority,"
and yes, often they were.
but Groucho could lash out
against anyone.
he said Chico was lucky
he had two talented brothers.
he said Harpo thought he was
Charley Chaplin. "He wasn't."
Erin Fleming called Groucho
"Grouch."
"No, no," he told his family
about her,
"she loves me,
she really
loves me."
"Strange,"
he said to the audience,
"I always
went
for redheads."

[Schvartze (shvahr-ts uh; English shvahrt-s uh) noun Yiddish: Usually
Disparaging and Offensive. a term used by some Jewish people to refer to a
Black person.]

DECEMBER 21
　for Adelle

the day goes by
unremarked by
most: Solstice,
yes,
and longest night
but
for how many
years,
wedding

anniversary.
Dear Ghost,
do you still
remember
Foley Square
and the Cornell
judge?
it's late in the
day
but I have not
forgotten.
rest easy.
—is it not
the artist's task
to retrieve
the irretrievable,
to gather together
the irredeemably
lost.
goodbye
goodbye
again.

...

NEW YEAR

the turn
of a page
the fall
of a leaf
the catch
of my breath
as I sit
reading

EPI-LOGOS

I believe
that my analytical
capacities—
the desire
to explain,
to separate—
go hand in hand
with my "creative"
capacities—
the desire to merge,
to connect
unknowingly
with another,
the desire
to know
and the desire
not
to know
(quelle Comédie!)
equally active
though
contradictory
in my bizarre,
always whispering
and buzzing
un-"individual"
consciousness—
McClure the first
to notice
because the puzzle
haunted
him too.

...

—why do you always attack
the idea of poetry as
personal expression?
—because poetry is not

personal expression
poetry is the door
to the larger
life.
—which larger life?
—the one I saw
in 1955
in port chester, ny,
the one
that remains
the measure
of all
my heavens
and
hells

NOTES

"TATER FRATERABO" from "COLLISIONS"

"Tater Fraterabo" requires some elucidation. "Tater Fraterabo" is the creator of some deliberately screechy YouTube recordings. In my little nonsense poem, tater when preceding fraterabo rhymes with rotter. When it follows fraterabo it rhymes with gator. There's also a joke that no one except possibly Dana Gioia and Iván Argüelles will get at the end of my poem. Frater, Ave atque Vale = Brother, Hail and Farewell. It's the very moving conclusion of Catullus' elegy to his dead brother. In the later Church Latin, a v sounds like a v but in Roman times a v was pronounced like a w. We think Caesar said Veni Vidi Vici (I came, I saw, I conquered) but in fact he said Weni Widi Wici. That's how Vale becomes Wally. Brother, Hail and Wally.

"…of BROADWAY" from "COLLISIONS"

"LULLABY OF BROADWAY" (*GOLD DIGGERS OF 1935*):
https://m.youtube.com/watch?v=34KAShRPWCo&pp=ygUobHVsbGGFieSBvZi
Bicm9hZHdheSBnb2xkIGRpZ2dlcnMgb2YgMTkzNQ==

BIG DANCE:
https://m.youtube.com/watch?v=RT9L-
a8LCWI&pp=ygUdTHVsbGGFieSBvZiBicmlhZHdheSBiaWcgZGFuY2U=

A friend writes me that "Al Dubin was a bloated playboy who resembled Harvey Weinstein but he was also a poet-lyricist and avocational authority on Edgar Allan Poe and a great admirer of Baudelaire, Rimbaud, the *école Parnassienne*, and the French decadents."

"CHIP DEFAA'S CD, *THE GEORGE M. COHAN SONGBOOK*" from "COLLISIONS"

This poem appeared in my book, *Creative Death*. The CD is available at http://www.chipdeffaa.com.

BAUDELAIRE: LA BEAUTÉ

I follow my translation of Charles Baudelaire's "La Beauté" with a translation of the concluding lines of his equally famous poem, "Le Voyage." I felt that the themes of the voyage, the death-wish, and the intense desire for *the new* were all relevant to the poet's conception of beauty. I felt as well that it is necessary for the translator to at least suggest Baudelaire's form. One of the great tensions in his poetry is that between the classical forms he employs and the shocking content he presents. He is clearly aware of this problem and makes an attempt to abandon the classical forms by embracing the prose poem, even going to the extent of rewriting some of the formal poems as prose poems.

BAUDELAIRE: INVITATION TO THE VOYAGE

This is a translation of Charles Baudelaire's great poem, "L'Invitation Au Voyage." Baudelaire himself remarks that his title is a reference to Carl Maria von Weber's "Invitation to the Dance" ("to the Waltz"). Baudelaire's form clearly suggests a dance-like movement. The lines, "The world will hold / Itself in a warm shining," are an inaccurate version of the poet's "Le monde s'endort / Dans une chaude lumière," "The world goes to sleep / In a warm light." But the rhyme with "gold" was insistent and, I felt, necessary. Another voice (*"Fall / Asleep"*) interrupts and makes my lines a little more accurate. Baudelaire's poem rhymes oddly for me with Yeats's "Among School Children." In both poems, the woman symbolizes paradise, and the longing for paradise involves sexual longing for the woman; yet "possession" of the woman is by no means "possession" of paradise: Yeats: "Her present image floats into the mind— / Did Quattrocento finger figure it / Hollow of cheek as though it drank the wind"; Baudelaire: "your treacherous eyes" ("vicious" in my translation). In both poems too, the longing for paradise may be nothing more than vastly inflated libidinal energy—though both poems seek also to evoke the ancient tradition of erotic mysticism. (Interestingly, the poem immediately preceding "Among School Children" in Yeats's *Collected Poems*, "On a Picture of a Black Centaur by Edmund Dulac," has the line, "I have loved you better than my soul for all my words.") One thinks as well of the Jungian individuation process, in which one "falls in love" with another, yet the other, even when attained, is unsatisfactory: what one "wants" goes beyond anything that can be supplied by another person.

Baudelaire's notorious, extravagant misogyny ("La femme...doit faire horreur...La femme est *naturelle*, c'est-à-dire abominable") can be understood in this light (among others). In the Catholic church, the virginity of priests and nuns is in part an attempt to focus erotic desire entirely on a somewhat personified deity—personified in the tradition of *The Song of Songs*. In the secular version of that tradition, desire tends to be focused initially on an actual person, who becomes the springboard for desire for the deity. But the person and the deity are not identical, and at some point in the process, the person must be "abandoned." Baudelaire's misogyny is perhaps in part an attempt to "manage" that abandonment. In "Invitation," the poet is inviting the woman to join him in the contemplation of an ideal landscape which "resembles" her—to see herself as he sees her. But his designation of her as "treacherous" is a powerful attempt to distance himself from her, too—as, indeed, it is an attempt to distance the woman herself from her "actuality." The "image" she projects is not the same as the flesh and blood person, who nevertheless haunts the poem (bathed as it is in sunlight) with her "darkness." The maternal quality of the landscape suggests that the woman's "treachery" is linked to her sexuality ("[La femme] est en rut, et elle veut être foutue"): the poem is in this sense an attempt to transform autobiography into myth, "lover" into "mother"—an attempt that Baudelaire is well aware is foredoomed to failure: "*Là*, tout n'est qu'ordre and beauté, / Luxe, calme et volupté": it's only *there* that such things happen. In an interview the late James Broughton remarked,

> I think the way to happiness is to go into the darkness of yourself. That,'s the place the seed is nourished, takes its roots and grows up, and becomes ultimately the plant and the flower. You can only go upward by first going downward. I've never been afraid of losing my beautiful neurosis as a source of my poetry. (Laughter)

Reading my translation of this poem, a friend commented on wanting to read a biography of Baudelaire. I answered:

The problem with biography in connection with Baudelaire is that—as Paul de Man suggests in his book, *Blindness and Insight*—once you have it (and of course it's important) but, once you have it, you're really not much closer to Baudelaire's work than you were when you began. Biography in a sense vanishes at exactly the point at which the work begins—which is part of what is involved with what de Man calls Baudelaire's "allegorizing tendency." The work is not a "fullness," not an attempt to transform the life into words, but something closer to an emptiness, a void, a nothing—even a flight from the life. The work is in this sense "Satanic." In the Christian tradition, everything that is is good. Insofar as something is "bad," it tends towards non-existence. Milton's "rebel angels" are "on this side nothing": they *just* exist. Allegory multiplies meaning but annihilates materiality, as does, in Baudelaire's version of De Quincey, opium. In "Invitation" everything moves towards sleep, dream, not towards "life." Cf. Keats:

> My heart aches, and a drowsy numbness pains
>   My sense, as though of hemlock I had drunk,
> Or emptied some dull opiate to the drains

One minute past, and Lethe-wards had sunk....

"Poetry" begins at precisely the point at which the self plunges towards nothingness—sleep ("drowsy"), death ("hemlock"), inebriation ("emptied some dull opiate"—as in Baudelaire), forgetfulness ("and Lethe-wards had sunk"). This is from de Man's essay, "Criticism and Crisis" in *Blindness and Insight*:

> [This] statement about language, that sign and meaning can never coincide, is what is precisely taken for granted in the kind of language we call literary. Literature, unlike everyday language, begins on the far side of this knowledge...The self-reflecting mirror-effect by means of which a work of fiction asserts, by its very existence, its separation from empirical reality, its divergence, as a sign, from a meaning that depends for its existence on the constitutive activity of this sign, characterizes the work of literature in its essence. It is always against the explicit assertion of the writer that readers degrade the fiction by confusing it with a reality from which it has forever taken leave. "Le pays des chimères est en ce monde le seul digne d'être habité," Rousseau has Julie write, "et tel est le néant des choses humaines qu'hors l'Etre existant par lui-même, il n'y a rien de beau que ce qui n'est pas." One entirely misunderstands this assertion of the priority of fiction over reality, of imagination over perception, if one considers it as the compensatory expression of a shortcoming, of a deficient sense of reality...It transcends the notion of a nostalgia or a desire, since it discovers desire as a fundamental pattern of being that discards any possibility of satisfaction. Elsewhere, Rousseau speaks in similar terms of the nothingness of fiction (*le néant de mes chimères*)...[A]ll nostalgia or desire is desire of something or for someone; here, the consciousness does not result from the absence of something, but consists of the presence of a nothingness. Poetic language names this void with ever-renewed understanding and, like Rousseau's longing, it never tires of naming it again. This persistent naming is what we call literature...Here the human self has experienced the void within itself and the invented fiction, far from filling the void, asserts itself as pure nothingness, *our* nothingness stated and restated by a subject that is the agent of its own instability.

This poem first appeared in my collaborative book with Iván Argüelles, *Saint James*.

"W.B.Y."

I hear the line, *Nothing is true, dear love, nothing is true* as spoken in Yeats' voice. I wrote this poem partly in response to W.H. Auden's famous elegy for

Yeats. I believe that Yeats is largely absent from Auden's poem whatever its other virtues.

"THE ARTFUL DARGER"

Quotations from *Charlotte's Web* by E.B. White and from *The Secret Garden* by Frances Hodgson Burnett. Well-known outsider artist Henry Darger (1892-1973) lived his entire life in near-poverty and showed his life's work to no one. His primary achievement was *The Story of the Vivian Girls, in what is Known as the Realms of the Unreal, of the Glandeco-Angelinian War Storm, Caused by the Child Slave Rebellion*, an immensely long saga Darger both wrote and illustrated. The phrase "l'absente de tous bouquets" is from Stéphane Mallarmé's essay, "Crise de vers": when God says "flower," a real flower appears; when the poet says "flower," there appears "l'absente de tous bouquets," the one that is absent from all bouquets. This poem first appeared in my book, *LIFE*.

"AN INCANTATION FOR THE POET FRANCISCO X. ALARCÓN IN HIS SICKNESS"

Adelle and I performed this poem at a gathering for Francisco X. Alarcón on January 11, 2016 at La Bohème in San Francisco's Mission District. Francisco died on January 15, 2016. By the end of June, 2016, Adelle would be gone as well.

"PAIRINGS: LORCA"

All the phrases in the right-hand column are taken from Lorca.

"REQUIEM"

"poor evelyn nesbit": I heard the remark about Stanford White in an *American Experience* television program, "Murder of the Century."

"in the first hours of his sainthood": Jake Berry's phrase. Jake was referring to poet Larry Eigner (1927-1996).

"the soldier / caught in the mist," "the man does not speak at all" are references to Samuel Fuller's film, *The Steel Helmet* (1951). Samuel Fuller is the "film director" referred to. The western which looks like it takes place in Southeast Asia is Fuller's *Forty Guns*. I found the remark in the Praeger Film Library book, *Samuel Fuller* by Phil Hardy.

"Comme un voleur de nuit," "De l'enfant rose": passages from Émile Deschamps' poem, "*A une mère qui pleure*."

"As from omen we get ominous": passage from Rudolf Otto, *The Idea of the Holy*, trans. John W. Harvey.

"He dwells, says St. Paul": passages from Rudolf Otto, *The Idea of the Holy*.

An earlier version of this poem appeared in a book I published jointly with my friend, Iván Argüelles, *New Poetry from California: Dead/Requiem*.

"MAESTRO"

The film *Maestro* seems to be an attempt to create a new American hero: a multisexual one. But Bradley Cooper is no James Cagney, whose performance as George M. Cohan in *Yankee Doodle Dandy* caught the spirit of the man if not necessarily the biographical facts. In *Maestro*, Bernstein's wife tells him he'd better be careful or he'll be remembered as an old queen. Cooper looks concerned. With all due respect, I think Cooper should have curtsied.

APPENDIX:

SOME SPECULATIONS ABOUT THE WORK OF WILLIAM BUTLER YEATS

Many years ago, I was in Cambridge, Massachusetts attending Harvard Summer School. I was more or less obsessed with the writing of William Butler Yeats, and I had just finished reading F.A.C. Wilson's book, W.B. Yeats and Tradition. *I thought Wilson had little talent as a literary critic, but he had been allowed access to Yeats' library and the quotations in the book were fascinating. I was going on about some of my discoveries to a friend, who suddenly said, "You sound like Paul de Man." I said, "Who is Paul de Man?" My friend told me about his brilliant teacher. Later, I studied with Paul de Man at Cornell University. When the notion of "Deconstruction" began to become fashionable in literary circles, I realized that de Man's view of Yeats—considerably at odds with the views of Yeats scholars—fit very well with his interest in Deconstruction. Yeats has been a presence—not necessarily an influence but a presence—in my work since that conversation in which I found out who Paul de Man was. What follows is perhaps the best of the articles I have written about Yeats, and I thought it might be a good idea in this late book to let the reader in on exactly what I thought Yeats' work was about.*

Part of what fascinates me about Yeats is that his work became—rightly— immensely famous but, I believe, at the expense of being genuinely understood. The groundwork laid by Richard Ellmann in 1948 was immediately accepted and continues to this day, but it contains some serious misreadings of central poems. (Paul de Man remarked to me that he thought Ellmann's work was "bad biography and bad criticism.") I think what Ellmann wrote was taken up with considerable relief because no one wanted to deal with Yeats' many esoteric influences—with the highly prolific Madame Blavatsky, for instance. Here was one of "ours," a good academic rather than a religious fanatic, who took care of all that, who elucidated Yeats' complex, quasi-religious symbol system with great clarity. When Paul de Man implicitly challenged Ellmann's readings, he was immediately vilified by the Yeats industry. Two personal examples: Thomas Parkinson, who wrote two books on Yeats, said to me, "I wish Paul de Man had never written about Yeats." After F.D. Reeve and I had done a joint reading in Berkeley, we began to strike up a friendship and were writing back and forth. Encouraged, I sent him some of what I had to say about Yeats. He immediately ended all communication with me.

WILLIAM BUTLER YEATS, *THE TOWER: A FACSIMILE EDITION* (SCRIBNER)

I say to the musicians: 'Lose my words in patterns of sound
as the name of God is lost in Arabian arabesques. They are a secret
between the singers, myself, yourselves....'
> —W.B. Yeats, introduction to *King of the Great Clock Tower*,
> quoted in F.A.C. Wilson, *W.B. Yeats and Tradition*

In 1928—the year he turned 63—the world-famous poet William Butler Yeats published a slim, beautifully-produced volume called *The Tower*. Yeats had received the Nobel Prize in 1923, and the book was awaited with considerable anticipation. The book's title referred explicitly to "Thoor Ballylee," a derelict Norman stone tower located near Coole Park, the estate owned by Yeats' friend Lady Gregory. Yeats had purchased Thoor Ballylee in 1917. After the tower was restored, it became a summer home for himself and his wife, Georgie Hyde-Lees. T. Sturge-Moore's beautiful image on the cover of *The Tower* shows Thoor Ballylee reflected in the still water below it. The image suggests both Yeats' poetic self-reflection—the meditative quality of his verse—and the hermetic tag, "As above, so below."

The Tower contains some of what were to be the poet's most famous, most explicated poems: "Sailing to Byzantium," the title poem, "Meditations in Time of Civil War," "Nineteen Hundred and Nineteen," "Leda and the Swan," and— last but far from least— "Among School Children." Yeats critic M.L. Rosenthal called *The Tower* "Yeats' finest single volume," and the book became, Brenda Maddox tells us in *Yeats's Ghosts: The Secret Life of W.B. Yeats*, the poet's "first best-seller." Yeats himself was very pleased with *The Tower*'s reception. He wrote Lady Gregory that "*Tower* is receiving great favour. Perhaps the reviewers know that I am so ill that I can be commended without future inconvenience...Even the Catholic Press is enthusiastic." And he told Olivia Shakespear, "*The Tower* is a great success, two thousand copies in the first month, much the largest sale I have ever had...."

Seventy-six years after the first publication of *The Tower*, Scribner's has come out with a facsimile edition with an introduction and two sets of notes by Yeats scholar Richard J. Finneran. (Finneran has supplied us with notes to Yeats' notes as well as notes to the poems themselves.) What can this new volume tell us about Yeats? Are any new insights possible in the case of a poet who has been the subject of so much intense critical scrutiny?

The book opens with the famous opening line of "Sailing to Byzantium" — "That is no country for old men. The young..." —and those two terms, "old men," "the young," reverberate throughout the volume. In the very next poem,

"The Tower," the poet tells us that, though he is afflicted by "Decrepit age," he is nevertheless in some sense "younger" than he has ever been:

> Never had I more
> Excited, passionate, fantastical
> Imagination, nor an ear and eye
> That more expected the impossible—
> No, not in boyhood when with rod and fly,
> Or the humbler worm, I climbed Ben Bulben's back....

Recent biographers have pointed out Yeats' none-too-circumspect, extremely problematical philandering as he aged. Is the combination of "Decrepit age" and violent youth— "Excited, passionate, fantastical / Imagination" —to some degree an indication, even an exploration, of that philandering? "With the easy chauvinism of his time," Brenda Maddox writes,

> [Yeats] used his wife as business manager, nurse, real estate agent, hostess, editor, literary agent, and proofreader while allowing his sexual interests to drift elsewhere. One of his first affairs was with Dolly (Dorothy) Travers-Smith, an artist and scene-painter for the Abbey and the daughter of the automatic-writing medium Hester Travers-Smith. Yeats found Dolly "slim and red-lipped." Friends were amused to watch him one day at a party at Lennox Robinson's cottage try to put her in a trance.

How does this slightly ridiculous philandering—this "faithlessness" — register in his poetry, if indeed it does at all? *The Tower* has one poem, "The Hero, The Girl, and the Fool," which ends with the lines,

> When my days that have
> From cradle run to grave
> From grave to cradle run instead;
> When thoughts that a fool
> Has wound upon a spool
> Are but loose thread, are but loose thread.
>
> When cradle and spool are past
> And I mere shade at last
> Coagulate of stuff
> Transparent like the wind,
> I think that I may find
> A faithful love, a faithful love....

These lines suggest that "a faithful love" is something one can find only after death. Another poem, "The Gift of Harun Al-Rashid," seems to be a transparent tribute to the poet's wife George and her mediumistic abilities:

> was it she that spoke or some great Djinn?
> I say that a Djinn spoke. A live-long hour
> She seemed the learned man and I the child;
> Truths without father came, truths that no book
> Of all the uncounted books that I have read,
> Nor thought out of her mind or mine begot,
> Self-born, high-born, and solitary truths,
> Those terrible implacable straight lines
> Drawn through the wandering vegetative dream....

But "The Gift of Harun Al-Rashid" does not suggest that Yeats has any sexual passion for his wife. "Margot" —a poem written in 1934 but kept unseen until 1970, more than thirty years after the poet's death in 1939—is addressed to Margot Ruddock, one of various "out-of-control" women (Brenda Maddox's phrase) with whom Yeats had extra-marital affairs. It continues *The Tower's* theme of "young" mind and "old" body:

I

> All famine struck sat I, and then
> Those generous eyes on mine were cast,
> Sat like other aged men
> Dumfoundered, gazing on a past
> That appeared constructed of
> Lost opportunities to love.

II

> O how can I that interest hold?
> What offer to attentive eyes?
> Mind grows young and body old;
> When half closed her eye-lid lies
> A sort of hidden glory shall
> About these stooping shoulders fall.

III

> The Age of Miracles renew,

> Let me be loved as though still young
> Or let me fancy that it's true,
> When my brief final years are gone
> You shall have time to turn away
> And cram those open eyes with day.

Though the "tower," the central image of Yeats' book, surely has a number of implications—including the suggestion of the dwelling place of the isolated contemplative—one of its meanings is very obviously the erect phallus. We should note as well that, though Yeats and others have emphasized the historical implications of "Leda and the Swan," not only does this frankly sexual poem depict the revelation of the divine (the "marriage" of mind and matter) as a particularly violent rape: it depicts it as an extra-marital affair. The violent, history-making moment does not arise out of anything Zeus does with his wife; it arises out of his lust (however "indifferent" the god may finally be) for a young woman. Still another poem, "Owen Ahern and His Dancers," deals more or less explicitly with Yeats' "mad" infatuation with Maud Gonne's daughter, Iseult:

> I did not find in any cage the woman at my side.
> O but her heart would break to learn my thoughts are far away.

Both the figures of Leda and the swan are important images in *The Tower*. In "Among School Children" Yeats explicitly associates Maud Gonne with Leda's daughter, Helen—an association he made in many poems:

> I dream of a Ledaean body...
>
> For even daughters of the swan can share
> Something of every paddler's heritage....

(Since Helen's mother is mortal, Helen/Maud Gonne is *half* divine—but in her beauty she takes after her mother: she has "a Ledaean body.") The swan appears again in the climactic third section of "The Tower":

> the hour
> When the swan must fix his eye
> Upon a fading gleam,
> Float out upon a long
> Last reach of glittering stream
> And there sing his last song.

And in "Nineteen Hundred and Nineteen" Yeats writes,

> Some moralist or mythological poet

> Compares the solitary soul to a swan;
> I am satisfied with that—

In both these latter passages, the swan is an emblem of the individual (or "solitary") soul. From this point of view (swan as individual soul), the multi-leveled Leda story suggests the immensely problematical attraction of the soul (swan) to matter (Leda)—an attraction Yeats refers to in "Among School Children" as a "drug" whose effects eventually cause the resulting child to "sleep, shriek, struggle to escape." In "Leda and the Swan," the encounter between soul and matter is presented in a primarily mythological/historical context rather than in the context of the individual, but the results are similarly disastrous:

> A shudder in the loins engenders there
> The broken wall, the burning roof and tower
> And Agamemnon dead.

Swans in the context of faithfulness/unfaithfulness suggest an earlier poem which also deals with old age, "The Wild Swans at Coole"—the title poem of a volume Yeats published in 1919. "The Wild Swans at Coole," set at Lady Gregory's estate, is at once autobiographical, descriptive and visionary. An aging Yeats, remembering his youth, sees the swans "Upon the brimming water among the stones." "All's changed," he writes,

> I have looked upon those brilliant creatures,
> And now my heart is sore.
> All's changed since I, hearing at twilight,
> The first time on this shore,
> The bell-beat of their wings above my head,
> Trod with a lighter tread.

The swans' "hearts," he muses—as opposed to his own— "have not grown old":

> Unwearied still, lover by lover,
> They paddle in the cold
> Companionable streams or climb the air;
> Their hearts have not grown old;
> Passion or conquest, wander where they will,
> Attend upon them still.

The swans present an image of "a faithful love," one which maintains its allegiance to the divine. 1/ Yeats himself, on the other hand, has become increasing involved in the beautiful "wood of matter" which surrounds him— "The trees are in their autumn beauty, / The woodland paths are dry" —and, as a consequence, has moved further away from the divine. Here too he is "faithless."

As Paul de Man was the first to notice, shining through Yeats' naturalistic "imagery" is a notion expounded by the Neoplatonist, Porphyry (232/3 - ca. 305) in his *De Antro Nympharum*, a commentary on the Cave of the Nymphs episode in *The Odyssey*. Yeats knew Porphyry's essay through Thomas Taylor's widely-read translation, and he refers explicitly to it in the footnote about "the drug" in "Among School Children." He quotes extensively from the essay in "The Philosophy of Shelley's Poetry"—one of the essays collected in *Ideas of Good and Evil* (1903)—and there are unmistakable references to Porphyry in both Blake and Spenser as well as in Yeats' own work. Though Thomas Taylor "was ridiculed, even persecuted, for bringing to the attention of his age a philosophy so subversive to established values," writes Kathleen Raine in *Blake and Antiquity*,

> Coleridge delighted in Taylor's works, Shelley possessed them, Keats too reflected their influence; crossing the Atlantic, they were all-important in the American Transcendentalist movement. To Emerson and Bronson Alcott Taylor was, as George Russell and his friends later called him, "the uncrowned king."

Appearing in *The Witch of Atlas*, *The Book of Thel*, and in the third Book of *The Faerie Queene*, the cluster of symbols discussed in Porphyry's essay is one of the key items of literary Neoplatonism.

As described by Porphyry, the Cave of the Nymphs is a kind of half-way house for all souls about to be born or about to ascend to heaven; as such it is regarded as the source of all life, which is symbolized by "waters welling everywhere." One of its gates— "the gate of generation" —leads to the earth, and the other— "the gate of ascent through death to the gods" —leads to heaven. The first is "the gate of cold and moisture" —for "cold...causes life in the world" —and the second is "the gate of heat and fire." If we keep only these details in mind—and Porphyry goes on to add a great many others—we can see how the Cave of the Nymphs is relevant to "The Wild Swans at Coole." The "brimming water among the stones," for example, is Yeats' equivalent to the water welling among the rocks of the cave, and the two activities of the swans— "They paddle in the cold / Companionable streams or climb the air" —represent respectively the descent of the soul into matter through the gate of cold and moisture and, since air is a purer element than water, the ascent to the divine. Yeats often imagines this ascent as proceeding in "rings" or "gyres" and as accompanied by the sound of a bell—here, "the bell-beat of their wings above my head." (Cf. the bells in "Byzantium" and "All Souls' Night.") 2/

Was the cluster of images in Porphyry's essay a mere "source" for Yeats—something he transformed in the course of writing his poems—or was it something else? That question is another issue raised in *The Tower*. In "Among

School Children" the poet makes a careful distinction between two kinds of "images":

> Both nuns and mother worship images,
> But those the candles light are not as those
> That animate a mother's reveries,
> But keep a marble or a bronze repose.

This distinction between different kinds of "images" is no new thing in Yeats' thought. In "Symbolism in Painting," from *Ideas of Good and Evil*, he writes that "All art that is not mere story-telling, or mere portraiture, is symbolic,"

> and has the purpose of those symbolic talismans which
> mediaeval magicians made with complex colours and forms,
> and bade their patients ponder over daily, and guard with holy
> secrecy; for it entangles, in complex colours and forms, a part
> of the Divine Essence.

"If," he goes on, "you liberate a person or a landscape from the bonds of motives and their actions, causes and their effects...it will change under your eyes, and become a symbol of an infinite emotion, a perfected emotion, a part of the Divine Essence...."

The use of mere metaphor, he argues in "Symbolism in Poetry" (also from *Ideas of Good and Evil*), is not sufficient: "metaphors are not profound enough to be moving." Symbols "call down among us certain disembodied powers, whose footsteps over our hearts we call emotions...." Even Shakespeare is criticized:

> Shakespeare is content with emotional symbols that he may
> come the nearer to our sympathy, but if one is moved by
> Dante, or by the myth of Demeter, one is mixed into the
> shadow of God.
> ("Symbolism in Poetry")

"Shelley's poetry," Yeats insists in "The Philosophy of Shelley's Poetry," "becomes the richer, and loses something of the appearance of idle phantasy, when I remember that its images are ancient symbols, and still come to visionaries in their dreams."

The "images" which "animate a mother's reveries" are in the realm of "mere story-telling, or mere portraiture"; at best, they are in the realm of metaphor. Images which "keep a marble or a bronze repose" —sacred images such as the golden bird invoked at the conclusion of "Sailing to Byzantium" —have another purpose altogether and "call down among us certain disembodied powers."

Yeats' earlier poem, "The Dolls," from *Responsibilities* (1914), deals with the two kinds of images in a comic way:

> A doll in the doll-maker's house
> Looks at the cradle and bawls:
> 'That is an insult to us.'

The "oldest of all the dolls" describes the baby as "a noisy and filthy thing"; its appearance in the shop brings "disgrace" upon the dolls. Finally, the doll-maker's wife ends the poem with an apology:

> 'My dear, my dear, O dear,
> It was an accident.'

"The Dolls" demonstrates that Yeats was capable of seeing the comic side of his dilemma, but it is precisely the notion of the sacred-but-nevertheless-*embodied* (*non*abstract) *image* which allows the poet to escape from the situation he describes at the beginning of "The Tower":

> It seems that I must bid the Muse go pack,
> Choose Plato and Plotinus for a friend
> Until imagination, ear and eye,
> Can be content with argument and deal
> In abstract things; or be derided by
> A sort of battered kettle at the heel.

At the conclusion of the poem, the "learned school" in which the soul studies is not the "school" of Plato and Plotinus, with their "abstract things," but something closer to the "school" of Porphyry, with its insistence that Homer "has obscurely indicated the images of things of a more divine nature in the fiction of a fable"—its insistence that Homer was, in effect, in Yeats' terms, a Symbolist poet. Porphyry's term for Homer's sacred imagery is in fact, in Taylor's translation, "fabulous symbols" —a phrase which shows up in a horrific context when Yeats comes to write "Her Vision in the Wood." (Yeats' interest in finding a "school" is also something to be kept in mind when we arrive at "Among School Children": the title refers not only to the "children" the poet meets in Reverend Mother Philomena's Montessori school but to the poet himself, who is still looking for a proper "school." Cf. the line in "The Gift of Harun Al-Rashid," the penultimate poem of *The Tower*: "She seemed the learned man and I the child....")

At the conclusion of "The Tower," Yeats pours forth a number of what are for him "fabulous symbols":

> Pride, like that of the morn,
> When the headlong light is loose,

> Or that of the fabulous horn,
> Or that of the sudden shower
> When all streams are dry,
> Or that of the hour
> When the swan must fix his eye
> Upon a fading gleam,
> Float out upon a long
> Last reach of glittering stream
> And there sing his last song.

Nor is Porphyry absent from Yeats' list. The lines,

> I choose upstanding men,
> That climb the streams until
> The fountain leap, and at dawn
> Drop their cast at the side
> Of dripping stone....

in part refer back to an earlier, nostalgic passage in the poem,

> in boyhood when with rod and fly,
> Or the humbler worm, I climbed Ben Bulben's back
> And had the livelong summer day to spend,

but both the "fountain" and the "dripping stone" (not mentioned in the earlier passage) are details from Porphyry, "fabulous symbols" which show up often in Yeats. (The "dripping stone" is equivalent to "the brimming water among the stones" in "The Wild Swans at Coole.") Here and elsewhere, Yeats is attempting, through the use of "symbols," "to liberate a person or a landscape from the bonds of motives and their actions, causes and their effects" and to allow the person or landscape to "change under your eyes."

"Among School Children" is the poem in *The Tower* which has been most explicated and, to my mind, most misunderstood. I wrote about the poem at some length in my essay, "Yeats' Poetic Art" (available from the archives of my online column, "Foley's Books," in my book, *Foley's Books*, and in *The Yeats Eliot Review*, vol. 18, no. 4, April 2002). The problem of the poem is not so much old age as it is the difficulty of distinguishing between kinds of "images." Yeats' intense infatuation with Maud Gonne's beauty (her "Ledaean body") led him to believe that she was an embodiment of the divine—a "fabulous symbol." As she ages, however, she seems anything but such an "image":

> Her present image floats into the mind—
> Did Quattrocento finger fashion it
> Hollow of cheek as though it drank the wind
> And took a mess of shadows for its meat?

Indeed, the once beautiful, "Ledaean" woman now seems, like Yeats himself, a scarecrow: "Old clothes upon old sticks to scare a bird." Not something to attract a bird like the swan but something to scare it away.

In this context, the concluding lines of the poem take on a meaning which is very different from the one which is usually ascribed to them:

> O chestnut-tree, great-rooted blossomer,
> Are you the leaf, the blossom or the bole?
> O body swayed to music, O brightening glance,
> How can we know the dancer from the dance?

Are these lines the expression of "organic unity" that critics usually take them to be? Isn't a chestnut-tree (like any tree) an expression of the ultimate unity of leaf, blossom and bole? Aren't leaf, blossom and bole parts of the whole? Are the two aspects of Maud Gonne—her divinity and her humanity—in a state of harmony or are they in conflict with one another? Aren't the dancer and the dance identical, since we can experience the dance only *through* the dancer?

A bole is "the stem or trunk of a tree." A leaf is "one of the expanded, usually green organs borne by the stem of a plant." A blossom is "the flower of a plant, esp. of one producing an edible fruit...*The apple tree is in blossom*." (Definitions from *The Random House Dictionary*.) As time passes, as the tree "grows," we experience bole, leaf and blossom. But that is the point: *as time passes*. I think that the answer to Yeats' first question is *No*: his "great-rooted blossomer" is precisely *not* "the leaf, the blossom or the bole" —not the tree that exists in time. Rather, it is a "fabulous symbol" —something existing outside of time, or in a different temporal order from the human and the natural. The elevated tone of "great-rooted blossomer" (as opposed to the mere "blossom" of the next line) suggests the difference. The "great-rooted blossomer" is, in effect, *nothing but* a "blossomer." Unlike Maud Gonne, it never ceases to manifest the divine; it never grows old, and it constantly points to what Yeats calls in "The Gift of Harun Al-Rashid" "Self-born, high-born, and solitary truths, / Those terrible implacable straight lines / Drawn through the wandering vegetative dream."

The meaning of the chestnut image is suggested by a passage in Basho's *The Narrow Road to the Deep North*: "The chestnut is a holy tree, for the Chinese ideograph for chestnut is Tree placed directly below West, the direction of the holy land." The "great-rooted blossomer" is like those images which "keep a marble or a bronze repose." The organic tree, on the other hand, is an image like those worshiped by mothers—an image whose reflection of the divine is essentially mutable.

A similar distinction can be made between the dancer and the dance. "The dance," writes Paul de Man in "Image and Emblem in Yeats,"

is a recurrent emblem for contact with the divine; the
following early quotation describes it well: "Men who lived in
a world where anything might flow and change...had always,
as it seems, for a supreme ritual that tumultuous dance among
the hills or in the depths of the woods, where unearthly ecstasy
fell upon the dancers, until they seemed the gods or the
godlike beasts, and felt their souls overtopping the moon; and,
as some think, imaged for the first time in the world the
blessed country of the gods and of the happy dead"...The
"dancer" on the other hand...is associated with the symbol of
the "body" and appears as a real woman in the generated
world of matter, capable of giving the "pleasure of
generation."

Maud Gonne may well have functioned as Yeats' Muse—and may well be to
some degree responsible for some of his finest poetry. His "worship" of her
physical beauty may have led him to a kind of "perfection." At the same time,
however, that very quest meant that he had to abandon something—and it is that
"something" which is the great issue of his later poetry. Was Yeats' interest in
Maud Gonne spiritual or libidinous? What kind of "image" —what kind of
"body"—has been the constant subject of his work? "Her Vision in the Wood"
(from *The Winding Stair and Other Poems*, 1933) contains the heart-rending
admission that the poet's attempt to become an archetype— "to liberate a person
or a landscape from the bonds of motives and their actions, causes and their
effects" —ends in woeful failure; the poem even contains Porphyry's significant
phrase, "fabulous symbol," now not spoken in triumph but in despair:

> That thing all blood and mire, that beast-torn wreck,
> Half turned and fixed a glazing eye on mine,
> And, though love's bitter-sweet had all come back,
> Those bodies from a picture or a coin
> Nor saw my body fall nor heard it shriek,
> Nor knew, drunken with singing as with wine,
> That they had brought no fabulous symbol there
> But my heart's victim and its torturer.

"How can we know the dancer from the dance?" The line is not a mere piece
of rhetoric but a genuine, anguished question: the burden of the poem is that
Yeats has *failed to know* the answer to that question, and it has cost him dearly.

Despite his sixty years, Yeats remains at the end of "Among School
Children" not a figure of wisdom but a learner— "among school children,"
asking questions to which he has no real answer. His stance at the end of the
poem is no different than it was at the beginning: "I walk through the long
schoolroom *questioning,*" though it is true that our experience of the poem has
deepened our sense of the importance of that questioning.

Yeats himself remarked upon the "bitterness" he found in *The Tower*; bitterness is definitely one of the volume's themes:

> Death and life were not
> Till man made up the whole,
> Made lock, stock and barrel
> Out of his bitter soul,
> Aye, sun and moon and star, all...
> ("The Tower")

*

> Some violent bitter man, some powerful man
> Called architect and artist in, that they,
> Bitter and violent men, might rear in stone
> The sweetness that all longed for night and day...
>
> What if those things the greatest of mankind,
> Consider most to magnify, or to bless,
> But take our greatness with our bitterness!
> ("Meditations in Time of Civil War")

*

> All, all those gyres and cubes and midnight things
> Are but a new expression of her body
> Drunk with the bitter sweetness of her youth.
> ("The Gift of Harun Al-Rashid")

But "bitterness" and "sweetness" are merely two examples of Yeats' constantly oppositional thinking—what he calls his "continual oscillations" (quoted in F.A.C. Wilson, *W.B. Yeats and Tradition*); they correspond roughly to "this world" and "the next world." Cf. The remarkable concluding lines to "Demon and Beast" from *Michael Robartes and the Dancer* (1921):

> O what a sweetness strayed
> Through barren Thebaid,
> Or by the Mareotic sea
> When that exultant Anthony
> And twice a thousand more
> Starved upon the shore
> And withered to a bag of bones!
> What had the Caesars but their thrones?

There is perhaps an even deeper "bitterness" at work in *The Tower*. Yeats' language as he attempts to define the functioning of the symbol—the symbol "*entangles*, in complex colours and forms, a part of the Divine Essence"; symbols "*call down among us* certain disembodied powers, whose footsteps over our hearts we call emotions" (my italics) —suggests one of his primary themes: the descent of spirit into matter, often referred to in esoteric writing as "the fall of man" or "the tragedy." The many oppositions which inhabit Yeats' poetry are all versions of this primary opposition, this "tragedy," which, Yeats argues in *The Tower*, is ultimately not worth it: 3/

> Never to have lived is best, ancient writers say;
> Never to have drawn the breath of life, never to have looked into the eye
>   of day;
> The second best's a gay goodnight and quickly turn away.
>   ("From 'Oedipus at Colonus'")

>   *

> What youthful mother, a shape upon her lap
> Honey of generation had betrayed,
> And that must sleep, shriek, struggle to escape
> As recollection or the drug decide,
> Would think her son, did she but see that shape
> With sixty or more winters on its head,
> A compensation for the pang of his birth,
> Or the uncertainty of his setting forth?
>   ("Among School Children")

Yeats' conception of "the symbol" was in effect Porphyry's cave all over again. If the symbol could "attract" spirit to it—emulate in little the "fall of man" —it could also lead man back to the divine. But what if the symbol couldn't accomplish this? What if all that happens is merely the fall? Worse, what if the poem achieves not cosmic revelation but only self-awareness? In this context, the lines, "the tragedy began / With Homer that was a blind man" ("The Tower"), take on an added dimension. Was Homer "blind" to the consequences of his actions? If even the much-lauded "symbol" involves "the tragedy," what hope is there for literature? The first stanza of "Two Songs From a Play" concludes,

> And then did all the Muses sing
> Of Magnus Annus at the spring,
> As though God's death were but a play.

Is "God's death" not, as Yeats once hoped, a "symbolic talisman," a genuinely magical event, but merely an esthetic matter—"but a play"? Was that in fact the primary revelation of his poetry?

With *The Tower* Yeats begins a passionate exploration of his entire career which brings him finally to the perception of an intense, monumental *lack* of unity, to the realization of a fundamental confusion among his impulses—a confusion which is at best masked by his doctrine of oppositions. "Why should not old men be mad?" he asks in *Last Poems* (1936-1939),

> No single story would they find
> Of an unbroken happy mind,
> A finish worthy of the start.
> Young men know nothing of this sort,
> Observant old men know it well;
> And when they know what old books tell,
> And that no better can be had,
> Know why an old man should be mad.

In the introduction to *King of the Great Clock Tower* (1935), Yeats wrote, "I say to the musicians: 'Lose my words in patterns of sound as the name of God is lost in Arabian arabesques.'" The paradox of Yeats' poetry, of which he was fully aware, was that it was conceived not as self-expression but as divine song—a celebration of those "powers" which he sensed operating "behind" nature; *yet it was everywhere fueled by a transgressive and autobiographical impulse which he could not escape if he were to write the poetry at all*. This paradox is constantly present in Yeats' work, which remains tremendously exciting but which nowhere arrives at that "unity of being" for which some critics wish to praise him.

In Yeats' early work the poet is imagined as a "priest": "The arts are...about to take upon their shoulders the burdens that have fallen from the shoulders of priests" ("The Autumn of the Body," 1898); "We who care deeply about the arts find ourselves the priesthood of an almost forgotten faith, and we must...take upon ourselves the method and the fervour of a priesthood" ("Ireland and the Arts," 1901). In his later work the poet is a "wild old wicked man." Yeats' late "affairs" (not to mention his delight in "dirty stories") were, at least in part, an exploration on "the biographical level" of this lifelong spiritual paradox—a paradox which resulted both in great poetry and in a fearful spiritual enterprise which was anything but "unified":

> The intellect of man is forced to choose
> Perfection of the life, or of the work,
> Yet if it chose the second must refuse
> A heavenly mansion, raging in the dark.

("The Choice," from *The Winding
Stair and Other Poems*, 1933)

*

But Love has pitched his mansion in
The place of excrement....
                    ("Crazy Jane Talks with the Bishop,"
                    from *The Winding Stair and Other Poems*,
                    1933)

NOTES

1. In *W.B. Yeats and Tradition*, F.A.C. Wilson writes, "the bird is the traditional symbol for the purified soul...and Yeats employs it consistently in this sense. One thinks of his manuscript reference to the 'birds that I shall be like when I get out of the body'...." In "Meditations in Time of Civil War," the image of the "stare" is *opposed* to the image of the "honey bee." (The word "stare," which Yeats explains is the West of Ireland expression for "starling," is echoed in "Two Songs From a Play": "I saw a *staring* virgin stand....") Cf. "As at the loophole there, / The daws chatter and scream...." Footnote 2 below suggests the meaning of honey bees in "Meditations."

2. Yeats' early poem, "The Lake Isle of Innisfree," isn't usually taken to be one of the poet's more esoteric pieces, but a number of its details—the water, the honey, the bee and its hive, the color purple, the number nine, the beans— come straight out of Porphyry. Indeed, in the context of Porphyry, the repeated lines in "Meditations in Time of Civil War" — "honey bees / Come build in the empty house of the stare" —may well be ironic, even mocking. "The sweetness of honey signifies, with theologists," writes Porphyry, "the same thing as the pleasure arising from copulation, by which Saturn, being ensnared, was castrated."

3. In *W.B. Yeats and Tradition*, F.A.C. Wilson points out that, according to Thomas Taylor, Dionysus—who shows up explicitly in *The Tower* in "Two Songs From a Play" — "is a symbol for spirit in its descent into matter." Wilson quotes Taylor:

This fall...is very properly represented as a cruel
dismemberment and a disaster, for life in the physical world is
a curse. Dionysus could stand only to lose by abandoning his
true nature....

In falling, the soul "'becomes bound in body as in a prison.'" "The ceremony of cutting out the heart as a symbol of eventual resurrection," Wilson goes on, "dates back to Egyptian funeral rites":

> When Jupiter takes the body of the slain god from the Titans
> and commits it into Apollo's keeping, the myth represents the
> rescue of the spirit of man from a merely material existence....

YEATS

evasive,
he answered questions
deceitfully
like a politician...
love
fades

looking
he found her dark
hair
inescapable...
try as he may...
love
fades

God
addressed him
when he was a child
assuring him
of a lifetime of visions
and endless
love
he said, "God, I will love You always"
God
fades

for Angela Manly

REMEMBERING H.D. MOE

AH, David Moe
who is no mo
you gave my rep
a needed glint:
the first to mention me
in print
(June, 1985)

...

JACK FOLEY (1940—)

San Francisco Bay-area poet Jack Foley has published eighteen books of poetry, five books of criticism, a book of stories, and a 1300-page "chronoencyclopedia," *Visions & Affiliations: California Poetry 1940-2005.* With his late wife, Adelle, he became known for his multi-voiced "choruses," a practice he has continued with his new life partner, Sangye Land. He has presented poetry on Berkeley, CA radio station KPFA regularly since 1988 and is currently one of the hosts of KPFA's literary program, "Cover to Cover." He has received two Lifetime Achievement Awards, one from Marquis *Who's Who* and one from the Berkeley Poetry Festival, and June 5, 2010 was declared "Jack Foley Day" in Berkeley. In addition, he is the first recipient of the K.M. Anthru International Literary Prize from the Kerala, India magazine, *LITTERATEUR RW.* His most recent books are *Grief Songs*, a book dealing with his sorrow at his wife's death; *When Sleep Comes: Shillelagh Song*s, poems ranging from traditional to experimental verse; *Duet of Polygon*, a collaboration with Japanese poet Maki Starfield; the companion volumes, *The Light of Evening*, a brief autobiography, and *"A Backward Glance O'er Travel'd Roads,"* a psychobiography dealing with "the growth of a poet's mind"; and *Creative Death*, a book of poems. *Ekphrazz*, a collaboration with artist Mark Fisher, is forthcoming from Igneus Press. In 2019, poets/scholars Dana Gioia and Peter Whitfield published *Jack Foley's Unmanageable Masterpiece*—a book of essays discussing *Visions & Affiliations.* Poet Olchar E. Lindsann writes, "Jack Foley's constantly evolving and exploratory writing has been a mainstay of the American avant-garde for many decades, and his detailed histories of California poetic communities demonstrate an engaged poetic historiography." In 1994

Lawrence Ferlinghetti remarked at the conclusion of Jack's radio interview with him, "Jack Foley is doing great things in articulating the poetic consciousness of San Francisco."

...

I raise my right hand.
The man in the mirror
Raises his left.

Left to right, Al Young, Jack Foley, Ishmael Reed, Jerome Rothenberg, and Ariel Resnikoff. Behind Jerome Rothenberg is Oakland Mayor Libby Schaaf in red. Sonoma County Poet Laureate Bill Vartnaw is above Ishmael's head, in a black hat. Koret Auditorium, San Francisco Main Library, 12/02/18. Photographer unknown.

...

HOLLYWOOD
an elegy

I have just learned
that in the end
Walter Brennan
became so conservative
and so looney
he thought
John Wayne
was a Communist
sympathizer.

.

there is
mystery
and madness
in this wild space
of dreams
and money
and longing,
where the unreal
is measured
by box office
receipts.
Orson Welles
spoke of the movies
as a woman
for whom
he had conceived
an unbreakable
and endlessly faithful
amour fou.

.

and when Peg Entwistle
leaped to her death
from the H
on the
HOLLYWOODLAND
sign
did she
wish to escape

the cowboys, Indians, romances,
the manifold illusions—
the lies—
of the place
where she lived.
was it all
a gesture
towards the real.
"I am sorry
for everything."

.

Dear Mary Kerr, *
We are no longer
"A people of the book."
History is the movies.

      ***

FOR JERRY

to see the dark shadow take them one by one
old friends
of many years
enemies too, indiscriminate in this
this is part of your Golden Years...

and now that dear, important man, Jerome Rothenberg,
moves to the shadows.
we listened together to T.S. Eliot intoning *The Waste Land*
on my car radio,
both mesmerized.
when it ended, Jerry said quietly,
"Jesus, Eliot was a wonderful poet."
he kindly told me, though he didn't have to,
of someone who had been badmouthing me in Southern
California.
know your enemies.
know your friends.
there are some
who appear at times
only to betray
work

of heart
and head,
mal-laborators,
their task
only
to destroy.
Jerry was never
one of these.
dear friend,
I learned of your death
just after Sangye and I
had seen
Antonioni's great *La Notte.*
you enter the night
head held high
heart beating
borne on the wings
of the art you practiced
with such intelligence
and such expanse
of love.

Jerome Rothenberg 12/11/31-4/21/24

FOR IVÁN

> *"He had a very difficult life which he accepted. The steady soft glow of your friendship for him was a balm and your understanding insightful and frequent reviews were a gift to the community."*
> —Malcolm Margolin

isn't it just like you to die *a las cinco de la tarde!*
Bang ! Bang ! la vida la pinche vida, hombre !
         and the deserts rolling
like futile seas towards Las Vegas and points east
"You're not American, you're an Indian."
I met you something like forty years ago.
I knew Marilla from Park School
and I had told her that I knew Ishmael Reed a little:

"Oh. Ivan"—not *Iván* in those days—"would like to meet him."
And so it began. you gave me a book, I wrote you back.
"What you wrote was closer to what I think I'm doing than
anything else I've seen. You say you write poetry. Listen.
I'm doing a reading at Larry Blake's. Why don't you read with me.
If your poetry is half as good as your criticism, I'm sure
you'll be fine." and so it began and so it began.
I was completely unknown. had done no readings
except for one that Iván attended at CCAC. there, Adelle and I did
one of the choral pieces I was writing:
that the hummingbird's wings are of a remarkable rapidity
he had noted often—nothing could be done—the
shift of his breathing—
and hearing it you grew excited. then the reading at Larry Blake's.
I wanted to write something special for it—
something elegant & long—
and as I wrote it bit by bit I phoned you and read you
what I'd done.
"Is it all right?"
"Yes, yes, it is. Keep it coming." your beautiful voice
assured me. I was amazed. no one, literally no one
had ever even liked my verse. yet I had continued,
if no one else was subject to its power, at least I was.
and then there was Iván. we were a great success
at Larry Blake's. someone had made a poster
and there we were. a young woman
came up to me afterwards and singled out the long, special poem
I had written, "Sweeney Adrift."
"What a poem!" she kept repeating. "What a poem!"
Nancy Peters and Phillip Lamantia were there to hear Iván
but they heard Adelle and me as well.
"Something original," said Nancy about my choral piece.
"welcome to the house of failure," I had written in "Sweeney Adrift,"
"see these are the structural bases of the house
its beams and arteries
its artificial light its hands its vast appendices
who is
not here?
the range of things
delights us welcome welcome

see there is the door it opens for us
welcome"
yes.
suddenly that door of poetry opened

and it was all Iván's doing.
everything I have ever done
was in that moment
which I shared
with a man
who would be my lifelong
friend.
dear man,
do you remember our many
times in Saul's Restaurant and Jewish Delicatessen
in Berkeley?
"Are you going to say it again?" you asked.
"Yes, I am," I answered.
and when the waitress served me
my matzoh ball soup, I asked her, deadpan,
as I did every time a waitress
served me such soup,
"And what do they do
with the rest of the Matzoh?"
"ARGH," said Iván.
will you tell me in a dream
if there is matzoh ball soup
in Poet Heaven?
our times together
flood over me,
there was so much
and so much richness
in them.
"Do you want to hear a poem?" you asked.
"Of course," I answered
and you read me
something beautiful.
"THIS IS DEDICATED TO THE ONE I LOVE
on earth to say there are couples that don't match
and flames of equidistant breath their smoke release
the sign is higher than summer and the cipher
cannot be discerned all sites and directions weathered
and grasses of twilight lift weary shadows to a god
whose nature is as unknown as death and what's
to sacrifice if not the soul's plagiarized copy afloat
in clouds where sleep is buried and poetry too
descant and folio of vast unremembered lines"
your lines will be remembered
and because of you perhaps some of mine as well
and perhaps our friendship.

goodbye, my loving, wonderful friend.
I'll go to Saul's and order matzoh ball soup
and I will say, as I always do,
"What do they do
with the rest of the Matzoh?"
and I will hear your laughter
and your moan
and I will know
some things survive
even the dark, dark hand
of Death.

Iván Argüelles, January 24, 1939-April 28, 2024

---

* Mary Kerr is a filmmaker friend. See https://www.beatera.org/personnel.

PRAISE FOR *COLLISIONS*
AND FOR JACK FOLEY

COLLISIONS lives up to its title by acting as a literary particle accelerator, slamming two or more things together to see what mysterious energies are released and what enlightenment might be shed by the encounter. There's a reason Foley's subtitle describes these pieces as "violences." Many are poems in the traditional sense, whether formal or free verse (and he is equally adept at both modes). Mixed in, however, are essays, historical notes, cultural commentaries, translations, collaborations, what could almost be called journal entries, and even reviews: the first piece is a magnificent prose poem of praise for Frank Capra's *Mr. Smith Goes to Washington.* The poet's always lyrical voice expertly unifies these disparate elements. Everything becomes poetry when he says it. Underneath the voice, though, is the running theme of consciousness as a chordal phenomenon. There are many Jack Foleys represented here, and every man Jack of them is on a spiritual quest to understand the universe. The journey becomes ours as we read and peer over his shoulder in wonder, like watching an astronaut of the soul step onto a strange new world.
> —Kurt Luchs

Jack Foley is doing great things in articulating the poetic consciousness of San Francisco.
> —Lawrence Ferlinghetti, "Cover to Cover," KPFA radio

Jack Foley is our firebrand experimentalist and he holds his torch high so the reader can have more light.
> —Michael McClure

There is no one alive who has done more for California poetry than Jack Foley. He is the most important living person for California poetry…the leading man of letters of California.
> —Dana Gioia

One of American poetry's essential thinkers and practitioners.
> —Christopher Bernard, *Poetry Flash*

Jack Foley's constantly evolving and exploratory writing has been a mainstay of the American avant-garde for many decades, and his detailed histories of California poetic communities including *O Powerful Western Star* and *Visions and Affiliations* demonstrate [an] engaged poetic historiography.
    —Olchar E. Lindsann, *Rêvenance: A Zine of Hauntings from Underground Histories*

Foley is multilingual, multidimensional in performance and on the page...Very little poetry these days is as compelling or comprehensively challenging to the imagination. To really read this work is to be irrevocably transformed at some essential place—not to be cast adrift but to come home, to open heart and senses.
    —Steven Hirsch, *Heaven Bone*

To read this book is to enter the mind of a poet who embodies living history. At 83, his intellect is no less formidable than ever, while his accumulated knowledge and wisdom are at their peak.
    —Deborah Bachels Schmidt

You continue to do in poetry and ideas what you have always done: challenge our assumptions and force us to actually think.
    —Jake Berry

FROM THE PUBLISHER

Octogenarian Jack Foley's *Collisions* is a book at play in the forests of the mind. The opening quotation from Dana Gioia defines the book's understanding of consciousness: "Human consciousness is an unstable republic of conflicting impulses, instincts, and appetites in perpetual flux." *Collisions* is an attempt to honor that notion of the chaos of consciousness while at the same time giving the reader an experience of thought and feeling that is not so chaotic that it is overwhelming. It tries to tell the truth about the mind in a way that feels if not comfortable at least familiar: we too have felt that fire, that movement. The book asserts that the fundamental condition of poetry is words in motion, constantly dis/uncovering perceptions of the new. "Ecstasy seems to be linked to the instability of language." Familiar with the many forms of traditional poetry and comfortable with the making of new forms, Foley conceives of every living poet as an Orpheus attempting to rescue Poetry-as-Eurydice. If poetry to some extent reveals the ramifications of the poet's identity, it does so in the context of the coruscations of words whose flashes move beyond identity into something more. The book deliberately plunges us into mystery as everything collides with everything else. Foley writes to a fellow poet, "'Home' is where you belong but 'home' isn't anywhere: it is always a profound absence: 'sound, noise that reaches for the ever-receding light.' I think that, underneath all the 'influences,' is this deep longing which is always asserted and always denied." Baudelaire: "heaven or hell who cares / In the depths of the unknown to find something *new.*" Foley goes on: "I suggest in *Collisions* that whatever caused us to be here is not omniscient but engaged in a vast attempt to understand itself: our actions as a species—even our destructive ones—are almost entirely modes of self-reflection, attempts at self-discovery or self-revelation. From this point of view, each of us is an experiment in knowing."

www.ingramcontent.com/pod-product-compliance
Lightning Source LLC
Chambersburg PA
CBHW071025150426
42812CB00073BA/3486/J